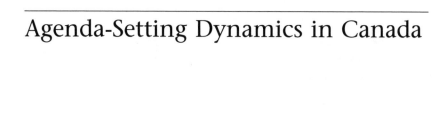

Agenda-Setting Dynamics in Canada

Stuart N. Soroka

Agenda-Setting Dynamics in Canada

UBCPress · Vancouver · Toronto

09 08 07 06 05 04 03 02   5 4 3 2 1

Printed in Canada on acid-free paper ∞

National Library of Canada Cataloguing in Publication Data

Soroka, Stuart Neil, 1970-
Agenda-setting dynamics in Canada

  Includes bibliographical references and index.
  ISBN 0-7748-0958-2 (bound); ISBN 0-7748-0959-0 (pbk.)

  1. Mass media and public opinion – Canada. 2. Mass media – Political aspects – Canada. 3. Public opinion – Canada. 4. Political planning – Canada. I. Title.

P96.P83S67 2002   302.23'0971'09048   C2002-910814-4

Canadä

UBC Press gratefully acknowledges the financial support for our publishing program of the Government of Canada through the Book Publishing Industry Development Program (BPIDP), and of the Canada Council for the Arts, and the British Columbia Arts Council.

This book has been published with the help of a grant from the Humanities and Social Sciences Federation of Canada, using funds provided by the Social Sciences and Humanities Research Council of Canada, and with the help of the K.D. Srivastava Fund.   11-20-02

UBC Press
The University of British Columbia
2029 West Mall
Vancouver, BC V6T 1Z2
(604) 822-5959 / Fax: (604) 822-6083
www.ubcpress.ca

For Kim and Sara

Contents

Tables and Figures

Tables

Figures

Acknowledgments

Public opinion data analyzed in this book were collected by the Angus Reid Group, CBC/*Globe and Mail,* Decima, Environics Research Group, Gallup Canada, and Pollara. The data were made available by the University of British Columbia Numeric Data Services, the Centre for the Study of Democracy (CSD) at Queen's University, and the Carleton University Data Centre.

Financial support for this project came from the Social Sciences and Humanities Research Council of Canada, in the form of a Doctoral Fellowship, and Nuffield College, Oxford, in the form of a Postdoctoral Research Fellowship. Some portions of this book were presented at the 1999 meeting of the Canadian Political Science Association in Sherbrooke, Quebec, at the 1999 meeting of the American Political Science Association in Atlanta, Georgia, and at Nuffield College. The end result has surely benefited from these discussions.

Moreover, both the UBC Department of Political Science and Nuffield College provided encouraging and stimulating environments for study and research. I am particularly indebted to those professors and students who offered advice on this project. These included Donald Blake, Kathryn Harrison, Richard Jenkins, Patrick Fournier, and especially Richard Johnston.

In addition, Bryan Jones and Byron Shafer offered indispensable advice along the way, as did Bradley Armour-Garb, Ken White, David Green, William Veloce, and my father, Lewis Soroka. I am also greatly indebted to Emily Andrew, Holly Keller-Brohman, and others at UBC Press for their help in preparing the final manuscript, and to my wife, Kim, who has been a constant source of encouragement and support.

Agenda-Setting Dynamics in Canada

1
Introduction

Public concern about unemployment tracks the unemployment rate, whereas the salience of environmental issues or the public debt is only intermittently related to real-world conditions. Why do media, public, and policy agendas move together on certain issues but not on others? To what extent can such trends be explained by real-world factors? To what extent are they the product of media effects, public concern, or attention from policymakers? These are the questions addressed in this book.

An appreciation of the different ways in which media, the public, and policymakers interact is central to our understanding of political systems. These interactions do not simply tell us something about politics – they *are* politics. This book, accordingly, focuses on these relationships. It represents one effort to understand (and model) the Canadian political system; in doing so, it seeks to contribute to our understanding of media influence on the public and policymakers, of the connection between the public and elected officials, and of the way in which everyday politics works in Canada and elsewhere. Evidence presented below suggests that a single, relatively simple *agenda-setting* framework is a particularly valuable (and considerably flexible) tool for understanding the day-to-day relationships between media, the public, and policymakers.

This book tells the story of eight issues – AIDS, crime, debt/deficit, environment, inflation, national unity, taxes, and unemployment – in Canada from 1985 to 1995. In doing so, it points to the value of using issues as a unit of analysis; the importance of drawing together work on media content, public opinion change, and public policymaking; and the strength of an agenda-setting framework in accomplishing both these objectives. To a large extent, this work can be regarded as a study into the value of an agenda-setting framework in investigating media-public-policy relationships. It asserts that, by using issues as the unit of analysis, an agenda-setting framework allows us to both merge disparate fields of political science and empirically map the structure of political communications.

The bulk of these pages is spent demonstrating that this is true, and the exposition involves a considerable amount of data gathering and model building along the way. Canadian media, public, and policy agendas are analyzed, as are the relationships between them. As a result, this study offers both a theoretical discussion of the agenda-setting framework and a demonstration of its use in modelling Canadian political communications. It is hoped that forthcoming analyses address more than just the agenda-setting literature, and that the results make valuable contributions to research on media effects, public opinion change, political representation, and the policymaking process.

The current work also makes an explicit effort to address both political science and everyday politics. This is perhaps the greatest advantage of examining issues – not only does this emphasis allow us to draw together political communications and public policy, but it also highlights the link between academe and the "real world." In short, the academic hypotheses and conclusions investigated here have readily observable real-world consequences.

Practically speaking, this investigation has two primary goals. The first is to empirically map relationships between the media, the public, and policy institutions in Canada using an agenda-setting framework – an issue-centred scheme that has informed well over 200 inquiries into interactions among the media, public, or policymakers.[1] Despite the considerable volume of agenda-setting research, however, this work still covers uncharted territory. Only a select few agenda-setting studies have allowed for multidirectional links between multiple agendas, few have done so with more than one issue, and few have dealt with Canada. Accordingly, this work is uniquely situated to observe inter-relationships between the three major agendas in Canada and adds new information to several ongoing debates in agenda-setting research.

The second goal is in large part a product of the first. Considering its use of an agenda-setting framework, this work has a vested interest in confirming the role of agenda-setting as a coherent and useful model of communications. That agenda-setting is either coherent or useful is still being debated, however. Although Rogers et al. (1997) imply that the agenda-setting paradigm was established with the first empirical study in 1972, a number of researchers have questioned the clarity of agenda-setting in general and the usefulness of "agendas" in particular (e.g., Swanson 1988).

It is certainly true that agenda-setting literature reflects an unfortunate combination of diversity and division. The flexibility of the agenda-setting framework is likely an indication of its potential, but reviews have seldom made coherent the varied agenda-setting literatures and hypotheses. The

---

[1]   Rogers and Dearing (1988) list 153 agenda-setting studies published before 1988. A brief search turns up at least another 100 published since that time.

second goal of this book, then, is to describe agenda-setting in a way that both draws together agenda-setting literatures and indicates the potential for this line of analysis in political science and political communications.

This chapter tries to fulfill the second goal by reviewing and synthesizing media, public, and policy agenda-setting research. There have been a number of recent attempts to describe the ever-expanding bodies of agenda-setting research (e.g., Dearing and Rogers 1996; McCombs and Shaw 1993; McCombs et al. 1995; Rogers and Dearing 1988; Rogers et al. 1993, 1997). The following history of agenda-setting literature draws in large part on these reviews, but makes an effort both to clarify important definitions and to develop an "expanded" model of the agenda-setting process. This expanded model serves as a guide for forthcoming empirical analyses and provides an integrative framework within which the different bodies of agenda-setting literature are combined and contrasted. Several authors have remarked on the divide that exists between media, public, and policy agenda-setting theory and research. This review, along with the empirical work that follows, is an effort to bridge the gap.

A Definition and History of Agenda-Setting Research

The study of agenda-setting is the study of issue salience – the relative importance of an issue on an actor's agenda. Moreover, it is the study of the rise and fall of issue salience over time, and of the relationships between actors' agendas. At a basic level, agenda-setting analysis seeks to draw empirical links between actors' agendas. As a body of literature, its more ambitious purpose is to track public issues and trace processes of political communication.

Agenda-setting research reaches across a wide range of political relationships, and the resulting diversity of agenda-setting work is both its greatest strength and most troubling weakness. Agenda-setting is certainly the only exploratory structure capable of incorporating mass media studies, public opinion research, and public policy analysis into a single framework. Swanson's criticism (1988, 604) that agenda-setting has suffered from "inconsistency of conceptualization, method, and result," however, points to the difficulties of such an integrative framework. Agenda-setting work is so varied and disparate that it is difficult for readers to assimilate even a small portion of what exists. Even simple categories are difficult for the reader to recognize – one author's "media agenda-setting" is another's "public agenda-setting," and so on. Despite the proliferation of agenda-setting frameworks, a single simple, integrative agenda-setting model continues to require definition and clarification.

The logical place to begin is with descriptions of the main components of agenda-setting work: "issues" and "agendas." Issues should not be confused with events. Shaw (1977, 7) notes the difference, suggesting that an event "is defined as discrete happenings that are limited by space and time, and an issue is defined as involving cumulative news coverage of a series of related events that fit together in a broad category." Events, then, are components of issues. A single robbery is part of the larger crime issue, or a particular policy debate on gun licensing is part of the larger gun control issue. An issue often comprises a large number of events; it might also exist over time almost regardless of the number of recent and relevant events.

Issues have been variously defined, as "a conflict between two or more identifiable groups over procedural or substantive matters relating to the distribution of positions or resources" (Cobb and Elder 1972, 82), for instance, or as "a social problem, often conflictual, that has received mass media coverage" (Dearing and Rogers 1996, 4). Issues need not be conflictual, however: there is no opposing side for issues such as child abuse, but child abuse is certainly an issue. Nor should issues be defined by the existence of media coverage. A media-based definition is logical only if one assumes that the mass media are always the first link in the agenda-setting process. When one does not want to make assumptions about the causal ordering of agendas, this becomes problematic. If a contentious subject exists on the public or policy agenda without appearing on the media agenda, is it an issue?

The answer is probably yes. Accordingly, the best definition of an issue is one of the simplest: "whatever is in contention among a relevant public" (Lang and Lang 1981, 451). "Contention" should be taken to mean that conflict may, but need not, exist. Rather, all that is required is an observable degree of discussion or concern. "A relevant public" is taken to mean not the "public" per se but rather a defined group relevant to the agenda-setting process. The relevant public might be the public at large, as measured through opinion polls, but it might also be journalists as indicated by measurements of the media agenda, or politicians and bureaucrats as indicated by measurements of the policy agenda. Additionally, the relevant public is not restricted to the "big three" agendas: in Dearing's description (1989) of the polling agenda, for instance, the relevant public is pollsters. Thus, an issue – valence or two-sided – can exist or originate with any actor in the political process.

Agendas, on the other hand, are "a ranking of the relative importance of various public issues" (Dearing 1989, 310). Issues vary in importance or salience relative to other issues – the order of issues, based on salience, is an agenda. An agenda, therefore, can be measured by making a list of issues in order of salience. Because issues vary in salience relative to each other, however, an agenda can also be measured by looking at the relative salience of a single issue. A measure of the public agenda, usually based on responses to the "most important problem" question, could include a list of issues in order of importance or simply the percentage of respondents citing a single issue.

Turning to the vast body of agenda-setting research, the most practical way to categorize past work is to sort (and label categories) based on the dependent variable. Accordingly, the resulting three bodies of literature are: (1) media agenda-setting, (2) public agenda-setting, and (3) policy agenda-setting (Rogers and Dearing 1988).

These three bodies of literature are both methodologically and theoretically related. Nevertheless, they have developed almost entirely separately from each other. *Public agenda-setting* has been developed for the most part by political communications researchers. Two sources are widely regarded as the theoretical roots of public agenda-setting analysis. The first is Lippmann's *Public Opinion* (1922), in which the author describes mass media's role in the relationship between "the world outside and the pictures in our heads." The second is Cohen's *The Press and Foreign Policy* (1963). Cohen is the first to state what has become the central public agenda-setting hypothesis: the press "may not be successful much of the time in telling people what to think, but it is stunningly successful in telling its readers what to think about" (13).

Following directly from Cohen's hypothesis, public agenda-setting research seeks to establish links between the relative salience of issues on the media agenda and the relative salience of those issues on the public agenda. The concentration on issue *salience* rather than issue *opinions* both distinguishes public agenda-setting research from the work that precedes it and tends to lead to much more successful results. Previous tests of media influence, most thoroughly described in Klapper's *Effects of Mass Communication* (1960), find little evidence of media influence on public opinion (see also McGuire 1986). Changes in issue salience, on the other hand, are more easily detected.

McCombs and Shaw's study (1972) in Chapel Hill, North Carolina, is widely regarded as the first empirical public agenda-setting analysis. These authors demonstrate a relationship between what survey respondents feel are the most important issues and the coverage these issues are given in primary news sources (print, radio, and television). Their results have motivated decades of public agenda-setting analyses, the cumulative product of which provides strong evidence of the original Chapel Hill hypothesis. The link between the mass media and public agendas has been shown to exist in studies that have been diverse both in their empirical methods – experimental and nonexperimental, cross-sectional and longitudinal – and in the subjects they address – for instance, the environment (Parlour and Schatzow 1978); pollution, inflation, and defence (Iyengar et al. 1983); home health care programs (Cook et al. 1983); energy and inflation (Behr and Iyengar 1985); civil rights (Winter and Eyal 1981); and the Gulf War (Iyengar and Simon 1993).

Cobb and Elder propose a similar framework for examining the policymaking process. In their initial *policy agenda-setting* article, they note the potential for this type of analysis to describe the means by which "an issue or a demand becomes or fails to become the focus of concern and interest within a polity" (Cobb and Elder 1971, 903-904). Their subsequent work highlights the impact of the media and public opinion on the state and national policy agendas (Cobb and Elder 1972).

Succeeding research uses an agenda-setting framework to look at the relationship between both the mass media and policy agendas (e.g., Gilberg et al. 1980; Pritchard 1986, 1992; Wanta et al. 1989) as well as the public and policy agendas (e.g., Flickinger 1983; Mayer 1991; Page and Shapiro 1983). A further variant examines issue dynamics within the policy agenda. This work, perhaps better termed *inter-policy agenda-setting,* surveys relationships between, for instance, the US presidential and congressional agendas (Andrade and Young 1996) or British political parties and policymakers (Kaye 1994). Studies by Kingdon (1995) and Baumgartner and Jones (1993) represent the current state of this line of research, combining policy and inter-policy agenda-setting hypotheses in their descriptions of the US policy process. Both deal with interactions between bureaucracies, officials, committees, and – to a lesser extent – the public and media agendas.

While public and policy agenda-setting are the most popular lines of agenda-setting research, there are also a small number of *media* or *inter-media agenda-setting* analyses. In truth, most media agenda-setting observations have taken place as by-products of public or policy agenda-setting studies. Gonzenbach's suggestion (1996) that the presidential agenda has a significant impact on the media agenda, for instance, is the derivative of a public agenda-setting analysis of the drug issue (see also Berkowitz 1992 and Wanta et al. 1989).

Research by Reese and Danielian (1989), on the other hand, stands as an explicit example of inter-media agenda-setting analysis. This research explores the relationship between the press and television, and finds that (1) television takes its cues on the salience of the drug issue from the press, and (2) the relative coverage of this issue by various media converges over time. Protess et al. (1985) note a similar inter-media agenda-setting phenomenon – the strongest agenda-setting effects of a newspaper's investigative series on rape, they find, are on the newspaper itself. Along similar lines, Soroka's (2000) inter-media agenda-setting work explores the link between entertainment and news media agendas.

In spite of the assertion made by Carragee et al. (1987, 43) that "a significant shortcoming of agenda-setting research has been its failure to examine the institutional framework within which the media form their agenda," the use of the media as a dependent variable in agenda-setting studies remains relatively infrequent. The few studies that do exist demonstrate the potential for and importance of media or inter-media agenda-setting analysis, however. These studies are the final link in the agenda-setting chain, connecting media, public, and policy agendas.

Towards an Expanded Model of the Agenda-Setting Process

A central goal of analyses in the chapters that follow is to integrate the three largely separate strands of agenda-setting research. Admittedly, this direction in agenda-setting analysis is not entirely new. Some policy agenda-setting work has dealt with both media and public opinion, although evidence tends to be anecdotal rather than empirical. Several public agenda-setting authors, on the other hand, have attempted to build a more complete empirical model of political communications by drawing together policy, public, and media agenda-setting fields. Rogers et al.'s study (1997) of the AIDS issue, for instance, explores agenda dynamics across media, policy, polling, and science agendas. Similarly, Gonzenbach's analysis (1996) of the drug issue examines relationships between presidential, media, and public agendas.

This broadened perspective demonstrates the primary advantage of the agenda-setting framework – its potential in linking media research and public policy analysis through a common vernacular and empirically comparable measures. This book aims to contribute along these lines. It draws impartially from media, public, and policy agenda-setting sources, and suggests that a combination of the different schools of agenda-setting research is both desirable and necessary. In order to both accommodate and take advantage of information in each body of agenda-setting research, however, the model of the agenda-setting process as it is presently understood must be updated and enlarged.

Models of the agenda-setting process have been explicitly described only intermittently. In most cases, authors imply relatively simple models, such as "media affect the public." There are a few exceptions; for instance, Rogers and Dearing's literature review (1988) includes an illustrated model of the agenda-setting process. These past models – illustrated or implied – tend not to adequately accommodate the vast agenda-setting literature, however. Perhaps more important, most are based on a view of causal links between the various agendas that is too restrictive.

A short review of agenda-setting research illustrates the difficulty with restrictive views of causal relations. To begin with, there are six possible directions of causality among the three major agendas. These directions vary both in their power and in their plausibility, so analysts have tended to concentrate on certain links and ignore others. Nevertheless, all of these links have been examined in one study or another, and the cumulative results point to the importance of taking each into account in models of the agenda-setting process.

The multidirectionality of the media-policy link is well documented. For instance, while Mayer's analysis (1991) of consumer issues reveals a rise in salience on the policy agenda preceding the rise in salience for the media, both Cook et al. (1983) and Protess et al. (1987) find that media reports – on home health care fraud and toxic waste, respectively – affect the salience of those issues for policymakers. Wanta et al. (1989) find similar examples of causal relationships running in both directions between the State of the Union address and the media agenda.

These findings are supported by studies of both the policy and the news-gathering processes. The latter indicate the significant role policymakers play as media sources – journalists often rely on government spokespersons and bureaucrats for quick, reliable information (Ericson et al. 1989). As a consequence, there is the distinct possibility that policymakers can affect the media content. Analyses of the policy process, on the other hand, suggest that the media play a role in setting policy agendas (Cook 1988; Kingdon 1995; Miller 1978; Mollenhoff 1965; Sullivan et al. 1993; Weiss 1974). Accumulated evidence, then, suggests that there is no single direction of influence between the media and policy agendas.

Evidence of multidirectional influence in the media-public link has been less clear. Certainly, the possibility of media influence on the public received considerable attention before the opposite relationship was hypothesized and examined. Nevertheless, there is evidence of public influence on the media agenda. Behr and Iyengar (1985) find evidence of a "feedback effect" for inflation, although results for other issues suggests that effects are more typically unidirectional. Neuman and Fryling (1985, 231-32) find much stronger support for bi-directional causality – their survey of ten issues finds "evidence of every pattern except consistent media agenda-setting. By far, the most dominant pattern was Interactive Feedback."

Other public agenda-setting research provides additional evidence that media-public effects may be bi-directional. For instance, Brosius and Kepplinger (1990) find that the direction of influence between German media and the public agendas varies depending on the issue. The authors suggest that the media tend to influence the public when television coverage is very intense; when there is a slow increase in issue salience, public opinion seems to precede issue salience for the media. In his survey of the drug issue, Gonzenbach (1992) finds it difficult to discern a single direction of causality; he suggests that the media can lead or be led at different times on the same issue. In sum, there is considerable evidence that the direction of causality in the media-public relationship cannot be assumed.

These issues of causality are taken into account in the expanded model of the agenda-setting process illustrated in Figure 1.1. The three primary agendas are shown, and causal arrows run in both directions between most of these agendas. There is no direct link from the policy to the public agenda,

Figure 1.1

An expanded model of the agenda-setting process

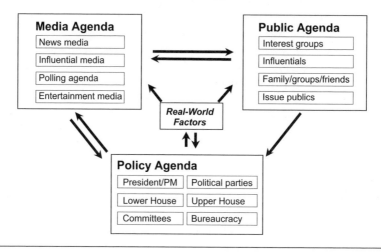

on the assumption that policymakers can affect the public through the media or real-world factors but not directly. Real-world factors are located at the centre, affected by policymakers and affecting each of the three agendas.

A number of subagendas are shown within each of the primary agendas. These lists are not intended to be comprehensive, but they do illustrate how the model accommodates both intra- and inter-agenda analyses. The effects of the *New York Times* on the media agenda are represented in this model in the same way as the effects of committees on the House of Commons agenda. More importantly, both these intra-agenda analyses are incorporated into a model of inter-agenda dynamics. Thus, the model accomplishes two tasks: (1) it provides a framework with which to compare, contrast, and combine a wide variety of agenda-setting analyses, and (2) it makes few assumptions about directions of causality, emphasizing the possibility of multidirectional agenda-setting and suggesting a structure for empirical investigation.

Figure 1.1 illustrates the agenda-setting model upon which the research described in this book is based. Assumptions are not made about the direction of causality; rather, statistical modelling is used to measure the significance of each of the causal links. All possible directions of causality are thereby measured and controlled for, with the aim of adding to current discussions surrounding agenda-setting causality and the wider agenda-setting process. In this way, the present study seeks to demonstrate the potential of the expanded model, using it not only as a means of reviewing of past work but also as a working guide for empirical analysis.

Research Strategy

Succeeding chapters rely on a "natural history" (McCombs et al. 1995) research design, studying the salience of single issues using aggregate data. This approach has been popular in the public agenda-setting literature (e.g., MacKuen and Coombs 1981; Winter and Eyal 1981; Gonzenbach 1996) and has tended to provide more convincing evidence of agenda-setting than studies relying on either individual-level data or aggregated lists of issues.

The difficulty with aggregated lists of issues is that the wide variety of intervening variables in the agenda-setting process – including real-world indicators and personal experiences – make a comparison of the distribution of salience across a set of issues problematic (Erbring et al. 1980). Furthermore, the varying nature of issues can lead to vastly different agenda-setting effects and dynamics. Not only can the identification of agenda-setting effects be lessened through aggregate issue measures but the effects can be masked entirely if various issues have opposing dynamics (Winter et al. 1982).

Perhaps more importantly, a longitudinal design provides more powerful evidence of causality than a cross-sectional set-up. While McCombs and Shaw's analysis (1972) stimulated a considerable body of public agenda-setting work, the authors assumed a direction of causality that their cross-sectional analysis could not prove. The problem is relatively simple: when both agendas are measured simultaneously, there can be no discussion of what comes first and what follows.

Worded differently, the problem with a cross-sectional design is that it is, by definition, static, while the agenda-setting process is, by definition, dynamic. This lack of congruence between the dynamic agenda-setting process and cross-sectional designs has been noted by a number of agenda-setting authors, aware of the possibility that cross-sectional methods may fail to identify the significance of a relationship over time between two agendas (Behr and Iyengar 1985; Brosius and Kepplinger 1990; Cook et al. 1983; Hill 1985; Iyengar and Simon 1993; MacKuen and Coombs 1981; Watt and van den Berg 1981; Weaver 1991). Perhaps most telling is Brosius and Kepplinger's comparison (1990) of dynamic and static analyses of the same data. Using dynamic analysis, these authors found a significant relationship where none was found in their static analysis, lending proof to Zucker's suggestion (1978, 226-27) that "the best way to make claims about the media and public opinion is to look at changes in both over time, and to use small enough intervals so that it is possible to determine if changes in one preceded changes in the other."

Funkhouser (1973) was among the first to use a longitudinal agenda-setting design. This author compared a media content analysis with answers to Gallup's "most important problem" question each year from 1964 to 1970. His conclusions were based on simply "eyeballing" the data, but longitudinal analysis has since become much more refined. Recent studies have used statistical procedures such as ARIMA time series modelling (Gonzenbach 1992, 1996; Zhu et al. 1993) and Granger causality (Brosius and Kepplinger 1990, 1992a) to quantify movements and trends in the data. The development of advanced econometric procedures in political science makes a longitudinal analysis of agenda-setting dynamics especially attractive.

Unfortunately, researchers are rarely able to combine both a longitudinal set-up and individual-level data, since individual-level variables are rarely available over an extended period. Thus, while longitudinal analysis is most often well equipped to address "stimulus attributes" – those pertaining to the agenda setter, such as variations in the nature of different issues – it is poorly equipped to address "audience attributes," such as individuals' exposure to the media (Winter 1981). Panel studies have attempted to overcome the difficulty of tracing audience attributes over time (Roberts 1992). The amount of time and the number of observations necessary for a thorough analysis of stimulus attributes makes a combined study of both sets of attributes very difficult. Consequently, this has been attempted very infrequently, and with very modest success (Zhu and Boroson 1997).

The nature of the available data, then, is most often such that an investigator must decide which to examine, audience or stimulus attributes. In other words, researchers must often decide whether to examine causality or individual-level differences. The emphasis of this book is the former. This necessitates a longitudinal dataset with an extended time frame, and data availability forces the amalgamation of a wide variety of poll results. As a result, the dataset is not well equipped to examine audience attributes. With only a brief exception in Chapter 4, the analyses described here concentrate on questions of causality and on variations in stimulus attributes.

Synopsis and Prognosis

Agenda-setting has developed out of work by Cohen (1963), McCombs and Shaw (1972), and Cobb and Elder (1972) into a large and varied body of literature, documenting relationships between and within the media, public, and policy agendas. While most studies concentrate on a single relationship between two agendas, some recent work seeks to provide a more expanded framework. This book demonstrates the strength of an agenda-setting framework, capitalizing on the use of issues and agendas as the common conceptual threads linking media analysis, public opinion research, and studies of the policy process. Following this line of analysis, it examines links between media, public, and policy agendas through a longitudinal survey of eight issues in Canada; the resulting evidence is intended to fill several gaps and contribute to a number of ongoing debates in the literature.

Chapter 6 is the focal point of the project, and surrounding chapters offer theoretical, methodological, and empirical support. Chapter 2 offers historical backgrounds for each issue examined in subsequent chapters, and introduces a threefold issue typology. While directions of causality should be tested rather than assumed, there are certain trends that past research leads us to expect. Chapter 2 reviews these trends and suggests hypotheses that inform subsequent analyses.

The next three chapters examine media, public, and policy agendas individually. These chapters provide the methodological background to each agenda measure, but also capitalize on the data collected to test a variety of additional hypotheses. Chapter 3 investigates the extent to which there is a pan-Canadian media agenda, and explores the relationship between individual Canadian newspapers. Chapter 4 looks at interprovincial consistencies and differences in the public agenda. Chapter 5 examines various measures of the policy agenda. Little effort has been made to measure the policy agenda outside the US, and the nature of the Canadian policy process makes this an especially daunting task.

The next two chapters form the empirical core of the project. Chapter 6 estimates issue-specific models of the agenda-setting process, exploring similarities and differences in causal issue dynamics and examining the validity of our issue typology. Chapter 7 then builds on these results. It divides the study period into shorter intervals, for instance, looking for changes over time. Hypotheses about the age of issues, mentioned briefly in Chapter 2, are dealt with here. Chapter 7 also examines the US media as an additional exogenous variable. Chapter 8 concludes with a review of the results, some further hypotheses regarding an expanded model of the agenda-setting process, and some suggestions for future work.

Methodological questions and problems have been a dominant theme in the literature, and this book is no different. The way in which media, public, and policy agendas are specified has a significant impact on the results; accordingly, a substantial effort has been made to review past work, clarify expectations, and build measures that are both theoretically justified and empirically sound. Having described and tested the individual agendas, this study then goes on to test causal links between them. When are there agenda-setting effects? Which agendas are leading, and which are following? How do causal dynamics change from issue to issue? How do they change over time? These are questions answered in the succeeding chapters. The answers provide valuable information about issue dynamics, agenda-setting hypotheses, and the nature of political communications in Canada.

2
Issues and Issue Types

Despite its wide use, it is not clear that the assumption, that the news media's influence is the same for all sorts of issues, should be accepted without an adequate test. It actually seems more likely that the assumption is not true, and that the news media can influence public opinion about some issues more than others. Therefore, it would seem that a useful question to ask is under what conditions is the news media's influences on public opinion maximal or minimal.

– Harold G. Zucker (1978, 227)

Different issues will lead to different agenda-setting dynamics. This is apparent in any survey of past agenda-setting research – media effects on public and policy agenda-setting tend to be negligible for inflation, for instance, while environment consistently shows evidence of media effects. Nevertheless, relatively few analyses have considered the possibility that their results are fundamentally dependent on issue attributes. And those that have, while making important contributions to our understanding of agenda-setting, tend to consider only one or two facets of the link between issue attributes and results.

A central goal of Chapters 6 and 7 is to demonstrate just how strong and ubiquitous this link is. For the time being, this chapter establishes some expectations about the effects issue attributes should have on agenda-setting dynamics. It begins with the recognition that this study's natural history design enables a comparison of the behaviour of different issues over time. In spite of the recent prevalence of natural history studies in agenda-setting, however, only a select few have taken advantage of this potential. Most previous research has concentrated on a single issue, and methodological variation has considerably hampered cross-study comparison. The result has often been a lack of recognition of issue attributes and the sometimes implicit (and incorrect) assumption that all issues should act similarly.

In contrast, this study gives special consideration to selecting issues that will illustrate a variety of agenda-setting dynamics. Issue selection is based on a number of initial considerations. First, previous agenda-setting studies tend to use particular issues, and the analytical advantages of replication make these issues especially attractive. Second, issues that present very low salience or little variation in salience over the survey period should be avoided (Eaton 1989), although analyses in Chapter 6 will show that this study makes two exceptions. Finally, coding limitations have to be considered. Issues have to be coded relatively consistently throughout the survey period in public opinion polls, and have to be easily searchable with a limited number of keywords in periodical indices and *Hansard,* as well as in government reports, bills, and accounts. With these limitations in mind, eight issues are selected with an eye to maximizing variation in issue attributes: AIDS, crime, debt/deficit, environment, inflation, national unity, taxes, and unemployment.

Using these issues as test cases, this work asserts that differences in agenda-setting dynamics are most often products of differences in the issues themselves. This hypothesis is examined through the testing of a new issue typology for agenda-setting. The typology is based in large part on past issue attribute hypotheses, but includes significant changes, additions, and clarifications to what have typically been ad hoc approaches to issue attribute theory.

This chapter reviews past issue attribute hypotheses and sets out the new typology. Building on previous work, three issue types are described: prominent, sensational, and governmental. The chapter then concludes with case histories for each of the eight issues selected for analysis. These histories draw the necessary links between the issue typologies and the issues themselves, and clarify our expectations for subsequent analyses.

Previous Work on Issue Attributes

Winter et al. (1982, 1-2) are among the first to note that issue differences might mitigate the public agenda-setting process, writing that "issues vary in the amount of time necessary to bring them to a position of importance in public opinion." The timing of the media-public impact, however, is only one of the dimensions across which issues may vary. Indeed, public agenda-setting literature contains four issue-centred hypotheses about variations in media influence. Each hypothesis deals with different issue qualities; some have received considerable attention while others have remained virtually untested.

Obtrusiveness

Zucker (1978, 227) suggests that "the less direct experience individuals have with a given issue area, the more they will rely on the news media for information and interpretation in that area." It follows that the less obtrusive an issue is, the stronger media effects can be. As has been noted elsewhere (e.g., Watt et al. 1993), the obtrusiveness hypothesis is closely allied with the media dependency theory of Ball-Rokeach and DeFleur (1976), according to whom individuals will be more dependent on the media for issues for which they do not have their own sources of information. It follows that the potential for media impact increases for issues for which the public is media-dependent.

Zucker's data bear some proof of his hypothesis, although the evidence is only mildly convincing.[1] Newer studies provide more solid evidence. Huegel et al.'s analysis (1989) of individual-level data, for instance, shows significant media effects for an unobtrusive issue (foreign affairs) and no effects for an obtrusive issue (social security). Similarly, Zhu et al. (1993) find that the media's agenda-setting role is stronger for international issues, while social interaction is a more powerful predictor for domestic issues. Finally, several authors suggest that their lack of evidence of agenda-setting for a single unobtrusive issue provides support for Zucker's obtrusiveness hypothesis (Ader 1995; Atwater et al. 1985; Weaver et al. 1992).

A few studies have found evidence contrary to the obtrusiveness hypothesis. Behr and Iyengar (1985) find agenda-setting effects for obtrusive issues (inflation and energy), for instance. The lack of an unobtrusive issue in their study limits their ability to test Zucker's theory, but their evidence demonstrates that an issue's obtrusiveness does not necessarily negate the media's agenda-setting potential. Demers and co-workers present the most compelling evidence against the obtrusiveness hypothesis. Using a variety of issues, they investigate the effects of issue obtrusiveness on agenda-setting. They find no evidence for Zucker's hypothesis, but instead find mild evidence for the "cognitive priming contingency," which posits exactly the opposite effect – "personal experience with an issue enhances rather than assuages media effects" (Demers et al. 1989, 794). While the body of accumulated research tends to favour the obtrusiveness hypothesis, then, Zucker's hypothesis has not been unchallenged.

---

[1] Zucker (1978) suggests that pollution, drugs, and energy (during certain periods) are unobtrusive, and presents some evidence that each issue shows a public agenda-setting effect by the media. Crime – an obtrusive issue – does not show significant public agenda-setting. Unemployment and cost of living do show agenda-setting effects, despite their obtrusive nature. While Zucker notes the importance of including real-world indicators in an analysis of media-public effects, however, he does not include real-world indicators in several of his models. Zucker's calculation of Pearson's r coefficients is also suspect – he has a maximum of 16 cases for the six issues analyzed, and no effort is made to control for autocorrelation in the time series data.

Duration
In addition to his obtrusiveness hypothesis, Zucker suggests that the longer an issue is on the agenda, the less chance there is for media effects. This is due to two factors: (1) the public has a limited attention span, and (2) the longer the issue is on the agenda, the more people have made up their minds.

Watt et al. (1993) provide some recent evidence of this hypothesis, finding that the effects of issue obtrusiveness are mediated somewhat by the effects of duration. As a result, an unobtrusive issue that has been on the agenda for a very long time (in their study, the Soviet Union) shows weak agenda-setting effects.

Abstractness
Yagade and Dozier's abstractness hypothesis (1990) suggests that agenda-setting effects should be larger for concrete issues than for abstract issues. Since abstract issues are more difficult for the audience to visualize, these authors assert, the potential for media effects is diminished. The effects of abstractness are distinctly different from those of obtrusiveness: "Media coverage of an obtrusive issue exerts little effect on issue salience because the issue is already directly experienced by individuals. Direct experiences overwhelm the influence of media coverage. Media coverage of an abstract issue likewise exerts little effect on issue salience, because individuals find it difficult to attach salience to something they don't comprehend" (Yagade and Dozier 1990, 4-5). Yagade and Dozier determine the abstractness of an issue using specialized public opinion questions; they find that nuclear arms and budget deficit are more abstract than drug abuse and energy issues. Subsequent agenda-setting analysis confirms their theory – nuclear arms shows no agenda-setting effects whereas energy does.

The abstractness hypothesis has not received as much attention as obtrusiveness. Nevertheless, Wanta and Hu's analysis (1993) of agenda-setting for international issues offers some further evidence. These authors find that agenda-setting effects on the public are stronger for concrete international issues (such as conflicts or terrorism involving American citizens) than for abstract international issues (such as trade or news not involving the US).

Dramatic Events
MacKuen and Coombs are among the first to note that dramatic events play a significant role in the agenda-setting process. These authors built models that attempt to predict public salience for seven individual issues using media content analyses and real-world indicators. In doing so, they find that including pulse functions representing dramatic political events significantly improves their models' predictive abilities (MacKuen and Coombs 1981, 103-24).

The potential role of dramatism in agenda-setting has been clarified more recently by Wanta and Hu. In their study of international issues, they suggest that "international conflict stories or stories dealing with terrorism, then, should demonstrate the strongest agenda-setting effects ... Stories with little conflict, such as a story involving a trade agreement, should produce weaker agenda-setting effects" (Wanta and Hu 1993, 253). These authors' results – surveying fifteen categories of international news – provide evidence of this hypothesis.

Towards a New Typology

Each of the above hypotheses divides issues in different ways and has different predictions for the public agenda-setting process. The hypotheses are not necessarily opposed, however. In fact, the possibility of predicting the magnitude of public agenda-setting by the media may improve if the obtrusiveness, duration, abstractness, and dramatic events hypotheses are considered together.

This has generally not been the case in previous work. In fact, there have been only two attempts to investigate more than one issue attribute hypothesis simultaneously. In the first, Zucker (1978) introduces and tests obtrusiveness and duration together. His tests lacked rigour, however, and only the former hypothesis has received attention since. More recently, Wanta and Hu (1993) investigate both the abstractness and dramatic events hypotheses. Unfortunately, their use of only unobtrusive issues precludes an analysis of Zucker's major hypothesis.

If combining the preceding hypotheses is one way to improve issue attribute theory, a consideration of the policy agenda is undoubtedly a second. Each of the preceding hypotheses, after all, deals with only two of the three major agendas. And just as public agenda-setting hypotheses have ignored the policy agenda, so too has the policy agenda-setting literature ignored the possibility that differences in policy agenda-setting may be a product of issue attributes. This is certainly not a justifiable omission – government agenda-setting by the media or the public should not for any foreseeable reason be immune to variation due to issue characteristics.

Further work on these issue attribute hypotheses, then, is motivated by three facts: (1) evidence varies for the obtrusiveness hypothesis and is scant for the other hypotheses, (2) there is a strong possibility that using the various hypotheses in tandem will improve predictions of agenda-setting effects, and (3) no effort has been made to establish a theory of issue attributes that encompasses the entire agenda-setting process.

A combination of the obtrusiveness, abstractness, and dramatic events hypotheses might proceed as follows. An issue is either obtrusive or unobtrusive. If it is obtrusive, the possibility for public agenda-setting effects is considerably diminished – the public will simply respond to real-world indicators. If an issue is unobtrusive, however, the possibility for and the direction of agenda-setting effects depends largely on whether the issue is abstract or concrete. An unobtrusive, concrete issue is prone to agenda-setting effects by the media, especially if this issue has dramatic qualities. An unobtrusive, abstract issue, on the other hand, is much less likely to show any agenda-setting effects.

This is not to say that an unobtrusive, abstract issue will never show agenda-setting effects. In fact, there are two scenarios in which this may be possible. First, as with an unobtrusive, concrete issue, dramatic events might cause an unobtrusive, abstract issue to show agenda-setting effects. Second, an unobtrusive, abstract issue might become more salient on the policy agenda. The effects of abstractness on the potential for issue salience are likely less powerful for the policy agenda than for the media and public agendas. Thus, an unobtrusive, abstract issue might show agenda-setting effects if it first becomes salient to policymakers.

This description illustrates the potential improvements that combining earlier hypotheses might make to the description or prediction of agenda-setting dynamics. The second scenario further demonstrates the potential importance of considering the policy agenda alongside the media and public agendas. A main objective of the new typology, then, is to take this into account.

Combining earlier issue attribute hypotheses suggests three most likely scenarios, or issue types. These scenarios are not necessarily mutually exclusive, nor are they exhaustive. An issue might demonstrate features of two issue types over time, for instance, and issues that show changes in salience on a single agenda without any changes on other agendas are not addressed here. Nevertheless, most issues will usually fit into a single scenario at any given time, and the scenarios likely provide a complete picture of the issue types for which there is any kind of agenda-setting effect. Each issue type is illustrated in Figure 2.1 and described below.

Prominent Issues
Prominent issues affect a significant number of people directly. They are both obtrusive and concrete. Real-world effects on individuals leave little room for either media or policy impact on public opinion; rather, issue salience is purely a product of real-world conditions. This applies primarily to the public agenda, but the situation is likely similar for the media and policy agendas. Prominent issues are real-world led, and – while interactions between the public, media, and policy agendas may exist – the predominant dynamic is between real-world phenomena and the three agendas.

Sensational Issues
Sensational issues are those that have little observable impact on the vast

Figure 2.1

Issue types

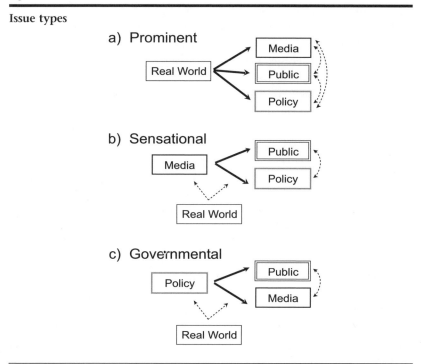

a) Prominent

b) Sensational

c) Governmental

majority of individuals. They are unobtrusive and concrete, creating the greatest potential for public agenda-setting by the media. This is the most significant feature of sensational issues: they are media-driven. The media agenda tends to lead the public and policy agendas. There may be a link between the public or policy agenda and real-world indicators, but this is largely incidental to the primary effect – the impact of the media. If real-world indicators have any impact (and they need not have), it is most likely on the media agenda. Often, this real-world impact is the product of a dramatic event, a particular incident that attracts the media's attention.

Governmental Issues

Like sensational issues, governmental issues do not directly and observably affect the majority of individuals – they are unobtrusive. Governmental issues, however, are not usually chosen by the media as significant. This is because the issues either do not present exciting or dramatic elements or are too abstract. A governmental issue can be concrete but, unlike a sensational issue, it can also be abstract, even while it is at the height of public salience.

Governmental issues become important to policymakers (including both elected officials and bureaucrats) before they spark the interests of the public or the media. The media may affect the public agenda for a governmental issue. This effect, however, is secondary: the media act primarily as a conduit for government-led issue cues. The policy agenda leads both public and media in this case. As with sensational issues, any relationship between the three agendas and real-world indicators is secondary to the effects of the policy agenda on the other two.

The Issues Themselves

Each of the individual issues analyzed in forthcoming chapters is described below. Issues selected for this study show some change in salience between 1985 and 1995, as well as relatively consistent coding in relevant indices throughout the study period. As discussed earlier, the sample of issues also provides examples of the prominent, sensational, and governmental issue types.

Issue descriptions include a brief history of the issue itself, an outline of government policy from 1985 to 1995, and a review of earlier agenda-setting work on that issue. This information is introduced here in part to justify the selection of issues. Moreover, it is included to provide issue-specific details that will be useful in later chapters, as well as examples of the three issue types and hypotheses regarding agenda-setting dynamics investigated in later chapters. Graphs of trends in issue salience for most issues appear in Chapter 6; readers who wish to compare the following case histories with time series graphs should consult that chapter.

Prominent Issues

Inflation

From 1985 to 1995 inflation in Canada falls into two periods. The first can be traced back to 1982, when the Bank of Canada abandoned inflation targets. "From 1982 to 1991, monetary policy in Canada was carried out with price stability as the longer-term goal and inflation containment as the shorter-term goal, but without intermediate targets or a specified path to the longer-term objective" (Thiessen 1998, 417). This method proved unsatisfactory, leading to a peak in inflation in 1989-91. The year 1991 marks the beginning of the second period: new inflation targets were introduced as part of the 1991 budget and inflation began to decline dramatically. In fact, actual inflation declined much more quickly than expected inflation during this period (Johnson 1997), reaching a low point in 1994 and then balancing out for the rest of the period.

Inflation has received a reasonable amount of attention in the public agenda-setting literature. Studies vary widely in methodology, making a direct comparison of results difficult. Nevertheless, evidence tends to point in the same direction: inflation is real-world driven, leaving little room for effects between the media and public agendas. Winter et al. (1982) present the only public agenda-setting study of inflation in Canada, indicating that inflation has a minimal potential for media influence. Behr and Iyengar (1985) find that (television) media attention is affected by changes in the consumer price index (CPI), and that public attention to inflation is affected by both real-world conditions and media attention. Demers et al. (1989) suggest that Behr and Iyengar's evidence of media effects is a product of using statistical methods poorly suited for longitudinal research, however. In their own investigation, they find no evidence of media effects on the public agenda for inflation above and beyond the strong effects of inflation itself. Finally, MacKuen and Coombs (1981) have a slightly more nuanced argument: real-world factors clearly drive public concern over inflation when inflation is high, but the media have a slightly increased role when inflation is low.

The bulk of earlier work, then, suggests that inflation is a prominent issue. The cost of living is experienced by everyone, every day; accordingly, it is most likely that there will be strong causal links between the CPI and public opinion. Other effects may exist, but these will be overshadowed by the effects of the CPI on all three agendas.

Unemployment

The 1985-95 period includes a fall and rise in unemployment in Canada, with the low point in 1989-90. This was also the high point for inflation, and the story for unemployment can be seen in part as a product of the same economic dynamics.

Unemployment insurance (UI, recently renamed Employment Insurance) is intimately linked to regionalism in Canada, and provincial involvement at various levels restricts the potential for major federally initiated changes to the program (Hale 1998). Changes are necessary, however, so the period from 1985 to 1995 saw a series of incremental amendments to various UI policies. The two most significant reforms during this period occurred in 1990 (Bill C-21) and 1995-96 (Bills C-11 and C-12).

Unemployment is analyzed in most of the same agenda-setting studies examining inflation, and results for the two issues are similar: no evidence is found of media effects on public opinion for unemployment in the US (Behr and Iyengar 1985; Demers et al. 1989; MacKuen and Coombs 1981) or Canada (Winter et al. 1982). Past evidence, then, overwhelmingly supports the idea that the unemployment issue is real-world driven. This is the case for the public, at least; policy and media agendas may be more susceptible to influence from other agendas, as investigated in later chapters.

Sensational Issues

AIDS

Acquired immune deficiency syndrome (AIDS), the life-threatening stage of infection with the human immunodeficiency virus (HIV), was first diagnosed in the early 1980s. Concern rose as AIDS spread rapidly, and by the mid-1980s there was growing recognition that, contrary to initial public belief, the disease was not restricted to the gay community. A series of public figures were either diagnosed with HIV or passed away from AIDS. Rock Hudson died in 1985, Freddie Mercury in 1991, and Arthur Ashe in 1993; Magic Johnson's diagnosis was made public in 1992. These cases helped make AIDS an increasingly important and public issue, along with alarming increases in the number of AIDS cases in many communities. A number of Canadian AIDS-related events also generated considerable press coverage during the period, specifically, the opening of the first AIDS clinic in Montreal in late 1985 and an international AIDS conference in the same city in 1989.

AIDS was clearly one of the most important new issues of the late twentieth century. That said, the response to AIDS in Canada was relatively muted, and there was no policy response before 1986. This late federal government response to AIDS despite the increasing number of diagnoses was partly the product of an ill-equipped bureaucratic structure (Lindquist and Rayside 1992; Desveaux et al. 1994), and federal funding of AIDS-specific programming announced in 1986 and 1988 continued to lack coordination and commitment. The Federal AIDS Strategy was finally announced in 1990, marking the beginning of a clearer commitment. This policy clearly lagged behind the spread of AIDS, however, which slowed around that time. It is not clear how attentive the public was to the AIDS crisis, nor is it clear to what degree government policy was in sync with public sentiment.

AIDS appears to have been a larger public issue in the US than in Canada, and its significance there has led to a number of studies examining AIDS on US media and policy agendas (e.g., Hertog et al. 1994; Dearing 1989). Rogers et al.'s study (1991) represents the most thorough agenda-setting analysis of this topic. Spurred on by the obvious and increasing significance of AIDS in the 1980s, Rogers et al. examine relationships between the media, policy, science, and polling agendas during this period. Various links between agendas are identified. Real-world indicators are shown to play a minor role: there is a weak connection between AIDS cases and the media agenda, but no real-world effect on any other agenda. This was likely a product of political recognition lagging far behind the spread of AIDS. The public agenda is not included in the analysis, although Rogers et al. suggest that a sharp increase in public concern in the mid-1980s is an indication of media effects.

AIDS, then, is an issue deserving further agenda-setting analysis. It has received attention in media and policy agenda-setting work, but no test has included public opinion. Furthermore, while the issue has been examined in the US, it has not been studied in Canada. Our 1985-95 study period covers a time during which AIDS should have risen from relative obscurity to significance on all agendas. A relatively small proportion of the population will have direct experience with AIDS, and a combination of rising numbers of cases (of almost epidemic-like proportions) and celebrity diagnoses make this issue one that is likely to draw media attention. Accordingly, AIDS will likely be media-driven and relatively unrelated to real-world indicators. It appears to be a good example of a sensational issue.

Crime
Public concern over rising crime has existed for decades, but it took on increased importance in the 1990s. This may have been due to concern about hard drugs such as cocaine and heroin, or to rising crime rates. Most types of crime, including violent crimes, have been declining steadily in Canada since 1991, however, whereas media, public, and policy concerns over crime have continued to rise. It is doubtful, then, that concern over crime is linked to actual crime rates.

Public concern might be connected to the prevalence of crime stories in the media. A number of authors, for instance, emphasize the mass media's predilection for crime stories, especially those that are sex- and violence-related. The US media are perhaps those most often portrayed this way (e.g., Davie and Lee 1995; Graber 1979; Sheley and Ashkins 1981), but the trend is also evident in other countries (on the United Kingdom, see Ditton and Duffy 1983; Smith 1984). A 1970 comparison of CBS and CBC news programs showed the US network to be considerably more oriented towards stories involving violence (Singer 1970). It is not clear, however, that this difference still applies. As early as 1979, Normandeau found that the volume and type of crime reporting in Canada encourages irrational fear and an inflated view of the frequency of crime, in line with US findings (e.g., Altheide 1997; Altheide and Michalowski 1999).

These hypotheses are in line with evidence of public agenda-setting for the crime issue. Several studies find that the increased salience of crime on the media agenda leads to increased salience on the public agenda (Einsiedel et al. 1984; MacKuen and Coombs 1981; Smith 1987). Whether the same effect will be found in Canada, using newspaper rather than television data, is not clear. The content of each medium has been found to be different, for instance, with television giving a stronger emphasis to crime- and violence-related material (Sheley and Ashkins 1981). Chiricos et al. (1997), for instance, found that television viewing leads to increased fear of crime, whereas newspaper readership does not.

Policy-centred work has also dealt with crime issues. A number of authors, for instance, suggest that the presence of crime and violence in the news media, especially on television, influences policymakers. This has been addressed from a media-centred standpoint, drawing links between effects on the public and effects on policymakers (e.g., Altheide 1991; Gilliam et al. 1996; Randall et al. 1988). It has also been identified in analyses aimed primarily at the policy process. A number of authors, for instance, have attempted to relate media coverage of crime to legislation or government spending (Scheingold and Gresset 1987; Pritchard and Berkowitz 1993). Pritchard (1986) suggests a further link between media coverage and the enforcement of legislation, finding that media coverage of criminal cases affects prosecutors' choices about which cases to take to trial.

No specific crime-related events stand out during the survey period. In terms of government policy and attention, however, crime has been a recurring and consistent policy issue. Furthermore, in the 1980s, while the Conservative government did not push forward the kind of crime policies common to US and UK neo-conservative governments of the period, political language on crime issues was clearly influenced by neo-conservative themes. Hatt et al. (1992) note that language turned from "justice and security" to "law and order" themes such as harsher penalties, individual responsibility, and morality. In the 1990s, crime received increasing attention in Parliament, accounting for growing numbers of both government and private member's bills. The change in tone and increased emphasis on crime may be connected with trends in the media and public agendas.

Thus, there was a considerable increase in the salience of crime from 1985 to 1995, and while the directions of influence are not clear, past work suggests that crime is most likely a sensational issue. Real-world indicators should play no role in the salience of crime, while the media should lead public sentiment. Policymakers might also lead the media and public agendas, however, if the change in policy approach occurs before changes in media emphasis. If crime rates do not drive the salience of crime, what does? The expectation here is that the media are responsible, but forthcoming tests should go some way towards answering this question.

Environment
Environmental issues have gone through two periods of increased salience. The first was in the early 1970s, marked by the first Earth Day in 1970. Environmental issues then virtually disappeared from view until the late 1980s and early 1990s. This period was marked by the crash of the *Exxon Valdez* oil tanker in March 1989, the twentieth anniversary of Earth Day in April 1990, and the much-touted June 1992 United Nations Conference on Environment and Development in Rio de Janeiro.

Environmental issues have received considerable attention in the agenda-setting literature, partly because they play the role of guinea pig in Downs's seminal "issue attention cycle" article (1972). Environmental issues do not visibly affect a majority of the population and are not intrinsically exciting. For Downs, these factors imply that environmental issues are prone to rise and fall in importance over time, rather than remain continuously salient. For agenda-setting researchers, these features suggest a strong potential for agenda-setting effects. Accordingly, a large number of public agenda-setting studies analyze environmental issues, and the evidence predictably supports agenda-setting hypotheses in Canada (Parlour and Schatzow 1978), Germany (Brosius and Kepplinger 1990), and the US (Ader 1995; Atwater et al. 1985; Hester and Gonzenbach 1995; Iyengar and Kinder 1987; MacKuen and Coombs 1981; Smith 1987).

The relationship between the salience of environmental issues and environmental indicators is not clear. The vast majority of studies have found no relationship (e.g., Ader 1995; Hester and Gonzenbach 1995). This makes intuitive sense: most indicators of environmental problems have moved very gradually over time while attention to the environment has experienced two brief periods of drastically increased salience. Blake (1999) demonstrates a relationship between environmental concern and local environmental conditions, however. His different results are likely a product of using smaller regions and a more nuanced measure of opinion on particular environmental concerns rather than the environment en masse. Blake's results, however, demonstrate that the role of real-world factors in the salience of environmental issues requires additional analysis.

At a national level, dramatic events are the most likely means by which to link actual environment indicators and their salience for the media, the public, and policymakers. The crash of the *Exxon Valdez*, for instance, undoubtedly influenced the media agenda. The actions of interest groups might provide a further link, albeit a less direct one, between reality and environmental concern. Environmental interest groups constitute the audience most attentive to environmental conditions, and action by groups such as Greenpeace is aimed, often successfully, at attracting media attention.[2] While these events may be able to account for intermittent jumps in the time series, however, they cannot account for a rise in salience spanning several years (1988-91) and a comparative lack of salience at other times.

In terms of the policy agenda, discussion of environmental policy in the federal government also reached a high point from 1988 to 1991. This was the period of the Canadian Environmental Protection Act (1988) and the formulation and introduction of the Green Plan (1990). The plan detailed federal environmental initiatives and objectives, and served as a guide for

---

[2] While the relationship between environmental interest groups and the media is not dealt with in detail here, it is well documented elsewhere. See, for instance, Pross (1992) on Canadian interest groups and the media, generally speaking; Anderson (1991), Neuzil and Kovarik (1996), Olien et al. (1989), and Rubin and Sachs (1973) on environmental interest groups and the media; and Brown and May (1989) on Greenpeace in particular.

federal behaviour until 1995. Hoberg and Harrison (1994) criticize the plan as being long on information dissemination and short on actual policy; regardless of its policy shortcomings, however, it is the most significant environmental policy initiative to date, in terms of both scope and fanfare.

The timing of this and other major initiatives suggests a relationship between policy, media, and public agendas. That said, the extended rise in salience of environmental issues from 1988 to 1991 remains unexplained. Harrison (1996) notes that environmental issues may not be able to surface when there are pressing economic issues. This is more an account of why environmental issues were not salient at other times than an explanation of why they were salient from 1988 to 1991, however. The time period studied here neatly brackets the rise and fall of environmental issues, and so this study is well equipped to examine what initiated this period of heightened salience. Most earlier work suggests that the environment will be the quintessential media-driven sensational issue, but the roles of real-world indicators and government attention require further testing.

Governmental Issues

Debt and Deficit

After declining gradually since the Second World War, federal government debt (as a percentage of GDP) began to climb again in the mid-1970s. This was in part a product of expansionary fiscal policy used to fight the effects of the first oil shock in the early 1970s and the recession in the early 1980s. The federal government was extremely lax in controlling its debt throughout the 1980s (Kneebone 1994). The debt was a significant economic problem by the mid-1980s, but politicians and the public recognized it as such only fleetingly in 1989 and not for an extended period until 1992.

Efforts to eliminate deficits and reduce the debt began in earnest with the rise of the Reform Party and the new Liberal government in 1993. Dodge suggests that political and public attention to the debt was limited in the late 1980s by the focus on free trade and tax reform: "Governments and the public can really only focus on one or two economic issues at a time" (Dodge 1998, 282). As a result, public attention and political will did not grow until the debt problem had worsened considerably. The height of concern over federal debt and deficits occurred after the period surveyed here, likely around the time of the 1997 federal election.

Debt and deficit issues have received moderate attention from agenda-setting analysts. Yagade and Dozier (1990) examine the abstractness of the deficit issue, although they do not look at the agenda-setting dynamics surrounding it. Weaver (1991), on the other hand, looks at public agenda-setting by the media and finds mild evidence of media influence regarding the public debt. More recently, Jasperson et al. (1998) find agenda-setting and framing-related evidence of media influence on public opinion about the US federal budget in the 1990s. Brosius and Kepplinger (1990) look at public debt in Germany and find different evidence from that of Weaver (1991) and Jasperson et al. (1998): in Germany public attention preceded media coverage for this issue. These authors suggest that this reverse effect is "likely to occur when problem awareness showed a long-term steady increase or decrease with little variation" (Brosius and Kepplinger 1990, 205).

The nature of the debt and deficit issue in Canada might create more dramatic agenda-setting effects. A gradually growing recognition of the debt problem does not appear to be an accurate account of the Canadian experience. Rather, public and political concern over the debt exploded, first briefly in April 1989, the month of the first budget discussion in which the debt and deficit slashing were identified as pressing concerns. The next stage of the debt/deficit issue began in 1993, with the budget of that year, the subsequent election, and the new Liberal government's action to eliminate deficits. As in 1989, this period of heightened debt/deficit salience appeared to have been brought on by government actors identifying the problem and staking a political claim. The debt/deficit issue, then, appears to be a governmental issue. The media agenda most likely affected the public agenda, but the media appears to have been led by policymakers, specifically, the Conservative government's 1989 budget speech, the 1993 election campaign,[3] and the Liberal government from 1993 onward.

National Unity
National unity is the single greatest recurring issue in Canadian politics. A brief history of the issue from its beginning is next to impossible. For this project, a synopsis of the issue from 1985 to 1995 will have to suffice. Even this ten-year period provides a considerable body of material.

There were several periods of heightened salience for national unity during the study period. The first was in 1987, with the conception of the Meech Lake Accord. The accord, designed primarily to bring Quebec back into the fold after the patriation of the Constitution in 1982, was to be ratified by each provincial legislature before 1990. In the interim, the salience of national unity issues waned somewhat for the public and the media, although presumably they remained important on federal and provincial government agendas. These issues were back in force on all agendas in 1990, however, when it became increasingly clear that the accord was in danger. It did not pass, leading to negotiations on the Charlottetown Accord soon thereafter. Unlike the Meech Lake Accord, Charlottetown was the product of a considerable amount of public discussion and input, and was to be put

---

[3] For more detailed information on issues in the 1993 campaign, see Jenkins 1999.

to a national referendum in 1992. These factors likely resulted in a pro-longed period of heightened salience for national unity issues, ending abruptly with the failure of the Charlottetown Accord in October 1992. National unity issues became prominent again with the (failed) Quebec separation referendum in October 1995.

Winter et al. (1982) offer the only public agenda-setting study of national unity in Canada, finding what appears to be a significant relationship over time between the media and public agendas. Their evidence is weak, however, and while the media may contribute to prolonging a debate, they are not likely to have been the source of national unity salience. This salience might have come from the public; it might be the federal government's response to changing opinion within Quebec on the Quebec-Canada relationship, for instance. Alternatively, national unity might simply be a governmental issue, one that is drawn to the forefront by government, subsiding when the attention of the government or the public moves elsewhere. This is the thesis implicit in Johnston et al.'s discussion (1996) of the 1992 referendum, in which the authors discuss government officials as the "agenda-setters" – it was government, after all, that initiated both the Charlottetown Accord and the subsequent referendum.

Like debt/deficit, national unity is likely to show governmental issue dynamics – the policy agenda should lead the others. Nevertheless, there is the possibility of effects elsewhere. The media may contribute to the discussion, and public opinion could lead as well as follow. Of the issues examined below, then, the agenda-setting dynamics for national unity are the most difficult to predict.

Taxes

Actual tax rates changed very little from 1985 to 1995. In fact, the average tax rates for Canadian families changed only 3% from 1969 to 1988 (from 34% to 37% [Vermaeten et al. 1995]). An examination of tax burdens – taxes collected as a proportion of GDP – reveals some change over time, although the magnitude of change is still both small and gradual. Drastic changes in the salience of tax issues during the survey period can probably not be attributed to changes in tax rates.

The salience of taxes did increase dramatically in 1989, however, with discussion about the Goods and Services Tax (GST), which was implemented in 1991. The tax created a considerable amount of political controversy throughout this period. It represented a major change in tax policy, placing the burden of the tax directly on consumers rather than producers and – perhaps more importantly – making what had previously been a hidden tax much more visible. The result was considerable public opposition to a policy that received considerable support from within the Conservative government.

The government's tactic was to stage a publicity campaign of immense proportions. Roberts and Rose (1995) describe the broad scope of this campaign, although they present only mild evidence of the campaign's success in changing public opinion. They suggest, however, that the government's GST campaign may have played an agenda-setting role, moving taxes higher on the public and policy agendas.

Tax issues have not been dealt with in previous agenda-setting analyses. Nevertheless, Roberts and Rose's work suggests the potential for considerable government impact on the media and public agendas; tax issues (from 1985 to 1995) should demonstrate governmental issue dynamics.

Summary

In spite of the potential for longitudinal studies to compare dynamics across issues, the vast majority of agenda-setting studies deal with only one issue at a time. Differences in methodology, country, and time period then conspire to make cross-study comparisons difficult if not impossible. As a result, the insights unique to multi-issue agenda-setting studies have hardly been examined. The current work tackles this problem by analyzing eight issues together, with a special emphasis on the potential effects that issue attributes might have on the agenda-setting process.

Accordingly, a central goal of this project is to examine and explain how causal links between the media, the public, and policymakers vary with issue attributes such as obtrusiveness, duration, abstractness, and dramatism. Previous issue attribute hypotheses have been combined above to create a threefold issue typology: prominent, sensational, and governmental. These issue types are not mutually exclusive or exhaustive, but they do provide a means with which to explain, and possibly predict, agenda-setting causality.

Theoretically speaking, the analyses in this book depend on this threefold issue typology. Empirically speaking, they rely on eight issues: AIDS, crime, debt and deficit, environment, inflation, national unity, taxes, and unemployment. Previous work suggests that each issue will fall clearly into one of the three groups: inflation and unemployment should be prominent issues; AIDS, crime, and environment should be sensational issues; and debt/deficit, national unity, and taxes should be governmental issues. The degree to which these classifications hold true is the subject of Chapter 6. Before models of the expanded agenda-setting process are tested, however, the next chapters examine the media, public, and policy agendas individually.

3
The Media Agenda

The five regions of Canada – British Columbia, the Prairie Provinces, Ontario, Quebec, and the Atlantic Provinces – all exhibit distinctive characteristics as far as their daily news profile is concerned. It is not too much to suggest that the differences of selection and stress involved [in press coverage] make it unlikely that persons in any of these regions can readily secure information in balance and context about the nation as a whole.

– Donald Gordon (1966, 158)

While analyses later in this book rely on there being a *Canadian* media agenda, it is not intuitively obvious that one exists. The above passage is testament to this fact, and Gordon is certainly not alone in his belief that Canadian media content varies widely. A review of past research reveals that most authors either assume or seek evidence that media content varies across Canada. The difficulties this suggests for the current study are obvious: if there is no pan-Canadian media agenda, questions about agenda-setting by the media at a national level are moot.

Accordingly, this chapter combines the necessary methodological discussion of media agenda measures with an investigation into whether there is in fact a Canadian media agenda. It begins by addressing the way in which the media agenda is operationalized. Using weekly or monthly counts of newspaper titles is certainly not the only way the media agenda can be represented, so earlier work is reviewed in an effort to justify this decision. Data are then used to test a variety of hypotheses regarding Canadian media agendas.

Searching for evidence of a pan-Canadian media agenda is the primary function of this analysis and, in contrast with earlier work that emphasized differences in newspaper content, the results suggest that one does indeed exist. Admittedly, this finding is aided by the fact that agendas are measured using a relatively thin content analysis – we are concerned only with issue mentions and completely ignore the more detailed content of articles. Nevertheless, a review of earlier work and of new evidence suggests that Gordon's charges are a little overstated.

In addition, our investigation provides an opportunity to address a number of related questions, including the potential effects of chain ownership and issue salience on consistency in coverage. The former appears to have no impact, but tests do suggest that issue salience has a sizable effect on the consistency of issue coverage across Canada.

Which Media Should Be Used?

As long as one is measuring impact on the national public or policy agenda, it seems logical to use major national media. Which national media is debatable, however. In the 1970s and early 1980s, many theorists agreed that "because of various characteristics television is not the best teacher of the relative salience of issues. The television viewer is time-bound and is forced to follow a series of reports presented in rapid succession. The newspaper reader, on the other hand, may attend to the newspaper fare in his own time, at his own pace, and can reread and reexamine the information made available by the newspaper. In addition, newspapers have the ability to repeat items more often over time" (Eyal 1981, 229). Newspapers, accordingly, have been used to represent the media agenda in a large number of public opinion (e.g., Benton and Frazier 1976; Erbring et al. 1980; Protess et al. 1985; Shaw and Martin 1992; Sohn 1978) and policymaking (e.g., Pritchard 1986) analyses.

The fact that a number of authors have settled on newspapers as their media agenda measure has not prevented others from using alternative measures, of course. Several have used newsmagazines (MacKuen and Coombs 1981; Stone and McCombs 1981; Yagade and Dozier 1990), although television network news programs have been the more frequent alternative. Spurred on partly by McCombs and Shaw's finding (1977) that television, unlike newspapers, displays no agenda-setting effects, those who believe firmly that television is a significant medium have sought to prove its agenda-setting significance (Behr and Iyengar 1985; Brosius and Kepplinger 1990; Cook et al. 1983; Hill 1985; Watt et al. 1993; Zucker 1978). The use of television network news as a media measure in Canada is extremely difficult for the time period in question, however. There is no index of television news programs in Canada before 1992, and certainly nothing comparable to the Vanderbilt Television Archives, upon which so many American agenda-setting analysts have relied. Television content, then, cannot be used as the media measure for this study.

There may also be theoretical reasons to avoid television, although these are decidedly weak. Carragee et al. (1987) suggest that the use of television content analysis to indicate which issues are important to the media is faulty, since television content simply does not concentrate on issues. Eyal (1981) notes that indices of television broadcasts include daily news broadcasts only, and ignore other politically relevant programming. The program *60 Minutes* in the US or *The Magazine* in Canada are obvious examples, but Eyal's criticism is especially interesting in the era of *Murphy Brown, Roseanne,* and *Ellen*. Both criticisms are hardly reasons to select newspapers over television, however. The first is not well supported by recent literature, and the second is more a reason to include entertainment media than to avoid analyzing television news. It is the lack of data, then, rather than theoretical judgment, that prevents the use of television content in this study.

Accordingly, the measure of the Canadian media agenda used here is based on a sample of major Canadian newspapers. Title searches, rather than subject searches, were performed individually for each issue in Canadian Business and Current Affairs (CBCA) and Eureka. Title searches were used because subject searches are susceptible to coding discrepancies in the indices, and preliminary tests showed that a considerable number of unrelated stories turned up when subject searches were used. The disadvantage of title searches is their assumption that the subject of an article is accurately reflected in its title, and this is not always the case. The volume of data necessitated a reliable search method, however, so title searches were used with the assumption that missed articles constitute a minor and random measurement error, and that changes in salience would be accurately reflected in the title search data.

Using title searches, then, series were recorded for each newspaper. These include the seven major newspapers covered by CBCA: the *Globe and Mail, Toronto Star, Montreal Gazette, Halifax Chronicle, Calgary Herald, Vancouver Sun,* and *Winnipeg Free Press. La Presse*, the only French-language newspaper for which data are readily available from 1985 onward (in Eureka), was also included. This selection of newspapers is broadly representative of both regions and owners, so combining them should produce an accurate indicator of the Canadian newspaper agenda.

Is There a Canadian Newspaper Agenda?

Before combining newspaper series into a single measure, however, we should explore the differences and similarities between individual newspapers' agendas.

Research into Canadian newspapers has been relatively scarce, but analysis thus far tends to emphasize regional differences. Two content analyses performed for the Royal Commission on Bilingualism and Biculturalism (1966) provide the most commonly cited empirical evidence on interregional differences in issue salience for the Canadian media. Bruce (1966) examines interprovincial variation in news about other provinces, and finds that, with the exception of news about Quebec, proximity to a province affects the amount of coverage given to that province.

Gordon (1966), quoted at the beginning of this chapter, offers a more comprehensive analysis. His content analysis of twenty-nine newspapers surveys a wide variety of national news subjects (15 categories with 49 subcategories) and compares content across newspapers in each of Canada's five regions for approximately six months in 1965. He emphasizes regional differences, suggesting that the gap between French and English newspapers is especially wide. This hypothesis, however, is based on observed differences in the attention given to various topics in all French versus all English newspapers. When results for the five regions are considered separately, it is not clear that Quebec always stands apart from the other four. Quebec clearly gives more attention to provincial politics and slightly more attention to biculturalism; for most issues, however, including federal politics, business and economics, agriculture, and foreign affairs, Quebec most often stands somewhere in the middle. Furthermore, when the rank orderings of the 15 major issue areas for English and French newspapers are compared, the results are remarkably similar (Gordon 1966, 54). Combining the English Canadian newspapers, then, both masks the variance within this group and overstates the divide between French and English Canadian newspapers.

Nevertheless, Gordon's interpretation of the data has been accepted by Canadian media scholars, most of whom continue to emphasize regional differences in media content. Elkin, for instance, writes: "The content of the English and French media, although basically following similar styles, often reflect different cultures. Different stories are given headlines in the English and French language press and sometimes the same events are treated very differently" (Elkin 1975, 235). More recently, Soderlund et al. (1980a, 1980b) compare the coverage of national unity issues in Canadian newspapers. They write: "It is rather widely held in Canada that there is no 'national agenda'; and that the rank ordering of salient events by the press differs by region and/or language" (Soderlund et al. 1980a, 349). While these authors interpret their own evidence as supporting this thesis, however, their data are no more convincing than Gordon's. The content analysis shows that bilingualism, the Quebec election, and Quebec language policy are more salient in Quebec than elsewhere. For a variety of other issues – such as Quebec separatism, air traffic control, and BNA Act patriation – inter-regional differences are insignificant.

While most studies emphasize regional differences, then, it is not clear that these differences necessarily outweigh the similarities, and certainly not clear that they preclude the possibility of a Canadian media agenda across a wide variety of issues. Furthermore, there is some evidence to support the idea of a pan-Canadian media agenda. For instance, several analyses of newspaper content during Canadian elections find evidence of a Canadian media agenda (Wagenberg and Soderlund 1975 and 1976; Wilson 1981; Johnston et al. 1992, 116). Surlin's study (1988) of Canadian and US television network news also finds no clear differences between English and French Canadian networks.

It is not clear that media coherency either during an election period or between television networks can be generalized to newspapers on a regular basis, of course. Elections may prove to be "focusing events" (Birkland 1997), creating more media coherency than exists during non-election periods. Television networks may be more restricted in their news coverage because of, for instance, medium-related limitations. Nevertheless, these findings do shed some light on the potential for a coherent, Canadian, non-election period newspaper agenda.

Exploring Inter-Newspaper Relationships

Time series for each of the eight newspapers are used here to test the existence of a Canadian media agenda. While subsequent chapters use monthly data, the analyses here use weekly series in an effort to increase the number of cases and provide a more nuanced analysis.[1]

Bivariate correlations represent the simplest way to measure relationships between individual newspaper series. With a number of newspapers for each issue, however, bivariate correlations do not provide a particularly space-efficient or illustrative means of presenting evidence. Moreover, the overall relationship between the newspapers is more germane to the following arguments than are correlations between each pair. While correlations were used in preliminary analysis, then, the explication below relies on a combination of Cronbach's alpha (α) and factor analysis.

Cronbach's alpha is a summary measure of scale reliability – the degree to which separate measures in a scale are related. Originally used as a test measure in designing psychological scales from cross-sectional variables (Cronbach 1951), it is used here as an indication of the degree to which issue salience in different newspapers rises and falls concurrently.[2] It is essentially a summary measure of the relationship between item variances.[3]

---

[1]   In preliminary testing, all of the following analyses were performed on monthly data as well. There were no significant differences in trends or results.

[2]   For a more complete description of Cronbach's alpha along with a more general discussion of reliability tests, see Carmines and Zeller 1979.

[3]   Cronbach's alpha is calculated as follows: $\alpha = N/(N-1)[1 - \Sigma\sigma^2(Y_i)/\sigma_i^2$, where N is the number of items, $\Sigma\sigma^2(Y_i)$ is the sum of item variances, and σ_i^2 is the variance of the aggregated measure. It is worth noting that the nonspherical disturbances in time series data bias confidence intervals but not the correlation coefficients themselves. As a result, alpha estimates should not be biased, in spite of the fact that it is a measure designed for non-time series data. For a more detailed discussion of the problems associated with time series data, see Appendix A.

Factor analysis provides another means by which to observe relationships between newspapers. Principal component analysis (PCA), a variant of the factor analysis approach, is the method used below. Factor analysis and PCA have been well described in statistics and psychology texts (e.g., Harman 1967; Jackson 1991; Jolliffe 1986; Lawley and Maxwell 1971; Rummel 1970), and since an accurate description involves a considerable amount of matrix algebra, PCA will not be described in detail here. Suffice it to say that PCA analyzes the covariance matrix of a set of variables (x_1, x_2, x_3, ..., x_p) and finds a principal component, y_1, which accounts for a maximum amount of variance. The process is repeated, finding further (uncorrelated) components, until p components are found. "Often the first few components account for a large proportion of the total variance of the x-variates and may then, for certain purposes, be used to summarize the original data" (Lawley and Maxwell 1971, 2).

The advantage of the PCA approach is that, while Cronbach's alpha provides a single indicator of inter-item covariance, PCA offers an indication of whether newspapers might be better represented in several measures. Moreover, by indicating how each variable is related to each component, PCA offers a more nuanced picture of the inter-relationships between a collection of variables – in this case, newspapers. In sum, Cronbach's alpha is used below as a general indicator of scale reliability: it speaks to the relationship between newspapers as a whole, and consequently the degree of confidence we can have when we discuss a Canadian media agenda. The PCA results are used to further dissect the relationships between individual newspapers.

Inter-Newspaper Differences in Canada

The first column of Table 3.1 shows Cronbach's alpha for the eight-newspaper measure, for each of the eight issues surveyed. Only data from 1990 to 1995 are used (to facilitate a forthcoming comparison with US data). The results show that issue salience is certainly not identical across newspapers in Canada. This is as expected: regional variation in story relevance and editorial decisions, among other factors, should prevent newspapers from following exactly the same paths. Nevertheless, the salience of some issues exhibits a sizable degree of consistency across newspapers. The alpha for tax issues in Canada is especially high (0.868), followed by those for environment and inflation. Debt/deficit and unemployment, on the other hand, reflect considerably more inter-newspaper variation in salience.

Based on earlier work, our first question is whether *La Presse* should be included with the other newspapers or whether there is a strong English-French divide in issue salience. The second column of Table 3.1 answers this question by presenting alpha values when one of the newspapers is excluded from the eight-newspaper measure; the newspaper excluded here

Table 3.1

Consistency in issue coverage in the media

	Canadian newspapers		US newspapers
Issue	Alpha	Alpha if item deleted	Alpha
Prominent issues			
Inflation	0.691	0.706 (*Globe and Mail*)	0.652
Unemployment	0.377	0.340 (*Globe and Mail*)	0.414
Sensational issues			
AIDS	0.504	0.502 (*La Presse*)	0.499
Crime	0.547	0.546 (*La Presse*)	–
Environment	0.635	0.640 (*Toronto Star*)	0.625
Governmental issues			
Debt/deficit	0.276	0.305 (*Winnipeg Free Press*)	–
National unity	0.611	0.746 (*La Presse*)	–
Taxes	0.868	0.868 (*Globe and Mail*)	–

Note: $N = 572$. Cells contain Cronbach's alphas, using weekly data for all Canadian newspapers from 1990 to 1995.

is the one whose exclusion results in the highest seven-item alpha value. Cronbach's alpha tends to be higher as N increases, so these seven-item results are not directly comparable with the preceding eight-item results. A higher or equal alpha value in the third column indicates a notable increase in inter-item consistency, however, since values in this seven-item measure are prone to be smaller.

The paper whose deletion leads to the highest seven-item alpha for AIDS is *La Presse* – excluding it leads to an alpha value of 0.502. There are, in fact, three issues for which issue salience in *La Presse* is the least linked with issue salience in other newspapers: AIDS, crime, and national unity. The difference for crime has no obvious explanation. AIDS and national unity, on the other hand, probably reflect regional differences. The first AIDS clinic in Canada was in Montreal, as was an international AIDS conference; these factors contributed to a higher salience for AIDS in Quebec newspapers. The fact that there is an English-French division in national unity salience also makes sense, since this issue should be more frequently and more dramatically salient in Quebec. Looking at bivariate correlations (not presented here), *La Presse* is most closely linked with salience in the *Montreal Gazette* for these two issues, providing evidence of these regional explanations. It is telling, however, that the *Montreal Gazette* is more closely linked with other English newspapers on national unity issues than it is with *La Presse*.

Regional Trends

The regional trends among Canadian newspapers are better observed through PCA, the results of which are reported in Table 3.2. Alpha values presented

Table 3.2

Regional and ownership trends in media coverage

	Prominent issues				
	Inflation		Unemployment		
Newspaper	1	2	1	2	3
HCH	**0.535**	-0.373	0.483	0.394	0.217
MG	**0.672**	0.052	**0.600**	-0.226	-0.337
GM	0.271	**0.778**	0.171	-0.595	**0.450**
TS	**0.600**	0.154	**0.536**	-0.186	0.150
WFP	**0.534**	-0.101	0.329	0.262	**0.492**
CH	**0.573**	-0.075	0.297	**0.596**	0.203
VS	**0.509**	-0.470	**0.370**	0.228	-0.621
LP	**0.661**	0.301	**0.644**	-0.311	-0.082
Eigenvalue	2.480	1.098	1.658	1.167	1.061
% variance	25.000	13.500	18.300	13.900	12.700

	Sensational issues					
	AIDS		Crime		Environment	
Newspaper	1	2	1	2	1	2
HCH	**0.429**	-0.422	**0.554**	0.050	0.499	-0.424
MG	**0.629**	-0.398	**0.446**	-0.342	**0.766**	-0.069
GM	**0.388**	-0.040	**0.504**	-0.094	0.403	**0.734**
TS	**0.589**	0.248	**0.541**	-0.238	**0.423**	0.079
WFP	**0.464**	0.405	**0.526**	0.208	**0.393**	-0.101
CH	**0.439**	0.331	**0.543**	0.362	**0.655**	-0.116
VS	0.423	**0.496**	**0.613**	-0.073	**0.576**	-0.436
LP	**0.637**	-0.380	0.045	**0.846**	**0.635**	0.477
Eigenvalue	2.071	1.064	2.022	1.080	2.497	1.171
% variance	25.900	13.300	25.000	13.500	25.900	13.300

	Governmental issues					
	Debt/deficit			National unity		Taxes
Newspaper	1	2	3	1	2	1
HCH	0.454	0.147	-0.487	**0.714**	-0.192	**0.750**
MG	0.539	-0.311	-0.097	**0.734**	0.001	**0.835**
GM	0.212	-0.394	**0.614**	**0.722**	-0.250	**0.567**
TS	**0.535**	0.218	0.092	**0.561**	0.488	**0.752**
WFP	0.399	-0.505	-0.427	**0.671**	0.151	**0.791**
CH	0.337	**0.653**	0.187	**0.685**	-0.246	**0.785**
VS	0.330	**0.400**	-0.019	**0.519**	-0.334	**0.742**
LP	**0.507**	-0.164	0.410	0.366	**0.774**	**0.842**
Eigenvalue	1.467	1.189	1.018	3.209	1.132	4.650
% variance	18.300	13.900	12.700	27.400	14.000	12.500

Note: $N = 572$. Cells contain factor loading from a principal components analysis, unrotated, using weekly data for all Canadian newspapers from 1985 to 1995. Text in bold indicates the factor loading for each newspaper for a given issue. Newspaper abbreviations: HCH = *Halifax Chronicle;* MG = *Montreal Gazette;* GM = *Globe and Mail;* TS = *Toronto Star;* WFP = *Winnipeg Free Press;* CH = *Calgary Herald;* VS = *Vancouver Sun;* LP = *La Presse.*

earlier are clearly reflected in factor analysis results. All newspapers load on a single component for taxes, the issue with the highest alpha coefficient. Other issues show varying degrees of inconsistency in coverage, debt/deficit and unemployment falling into three components.

In no case is there evidence of regional subgroups. Newspapers from the West, for instance, do not consistently load on the same component, and when they do it is often along with newspapers from elsewhere. It may be that concentrating only on major papers and having only one paper from a given province (with the exception of Ontario and Quebec) have yielded results that lack the detail required to pick up on regional trends. It is clear, however, that the present evidence cannot support the idea of regional subgroups. *La Presse* loads on a separate component for crime and national unity, suggesting that this newspaper follows a different trend from the English newspapers for these issues. For most issues, however, salience for *La Presse* is not markedly different from that for English newspapers. In sum, these results suggest a French-English divide in issue salience for crime and national unity, but no other obvious regional trends.

Ownership Trends

One might also expect newspapers to group together by ownership. The growing concentration (and often monopolization) of newspaper ownership has drawn a great deal of criticism, especially following the spate of mergers and acquisitions made by Thomson and Southam in the early 1980s (prompting the Royal Commission on Newspapers) and a series of Hollinger/ Southam acquisitions in the mid to late 1990s (Shaw and Thomas 1994; Winter 1997; Taras 1999).

Opponents of newspaper mergers suggest that concentration of ownership decreases variation in content (Bagdikian 1987; Herman and Chomsky 1988; Winter 1997), and the newspapers covered here could present a useful cross-section for observing trends in this regard. During the time period examined, the *Globe and Mail* and *Winnipeg Free Press* were owned by Thomson; the *Montreal Gazette*, *Calgary Herald*, and *Vancouver Sun* were owned by Hollinger/Southam; the *Toronto Star* and *La Presse* were owned by other media groups (Torstar, Gesca); and the *Halifax Chronicle Herald* was independent. The clearest ownership trend would be that the Thomson or Southam papers would group together in the factor analyses displayed in Table 3.2. This, however, is not the case. This is in line with the bulk of earlier research – despite suggestions that concentration of ownership leads to concentration of content, a variety of studies find no relationship between newspaper ownership and newspaper content in either the US or Canada (Coulson 1994; Picard et al. 1988; Wagenberg and Soderlund 1976). The evidence presented in Table 3.2 buttresses these earlier findings. There may still be a relationship between media ownership and content, but it remains unproven in quantitative analyses.

Inter-Newspaper Consistency in Canada: A Point of Comparison

A central difficulty with interpreting past evidence of inter-newspaper consistency in Canada lies in the problem of assessing just how much difference must exist between media sources before we know there are significant differences. Conversely, how much difference can exist without violating the assumption that there is a single agenda? We cannot expect that different newspapers will have exactly the same content, so a certain amount of difference must be allowed, but how much?

Evidence from the US might go some way towards solving this problem. It is widely held that there is a coherent US media agenda. The bulk of research in the US deals with the three major television networks, and these studies provide overwhelming evidence of similarity in network news content (e.g., Carroll et al. 1997; Fowler and Showalter 1974; Hester 1978; Riffe et al. 1986; Stempel 1985). Research using newspapers has come to similar conclusions (Danielian and Reese 1989; Stempel 1985). Unfortunately, the issues and methods of analysis in American studies are not the same as those found in Canadian examples, so the two groups are not directly comparable.

In an effort to address this problem, data were collected for AIDS, environment, inflation, and unemployment from several US newspapers from 1990 to 1995. US data were not collected for all series because either (a) some issues were exclusive to Canada and would not be reported extensively in US media (debt/deficit, national unity, taxes [including GST]), or (b) results from the US search engines were too large (crime). Nevertheless, data for these four issues should provide an adequate comparison of consistency in issue coverage in Canadian and US newspapers.

The US newspapers for which content analyses were done are as follows: the *New York Times, Washington Post, Washington Times* (Home Edition), *USA Today* (Final Edition), *Seattle Times, San Francisco Chronicle* (Final Edition), *St. Louis Post-Dispatch* (Five Star Edition), and *St. Petersburg Times* (City Edition). The selection of these newspapers was dictated largely by their availability from 1990 onward in the Lexis-Nexis search engine. Nevertheless, they do represent a reasonable sample of major US newspapers. The *New York Times* and *Washington Post* are widely regarded as leading newspapers in the US, and are consistently selected as representatives of the US media agenda in agenda-setting and media analyses. *USA Today* is the nation's most read daily, and – of these first three – is the one that aims most exclusively at a national audience; the other two combine national news with varying amounts of local/regional coverage. The *San Francisco Chronicle, St. Petersburg Times, Washington Times, St. Louis Post-Dispatch,* and *Seattle Times,* on the other hand, are large regionally centred papers, representing various regions across the country. All papers were searched in Lexis-Nexis using the same title search keywords as those used in the Canadian content analyses.

Returning to Table 3.1, the third column presents Cronbach's alpha for the US newspaper series. Since the alphas reported in the first and third columns are based on the same number of items, they are directly comparable, and a comparison indicates that it is incorrect to assume that Canadian media show an uncommon amount of inconsistency in coverage. In fact, for the four issues for which there are comparable US data, there are no notable differences between the Canadian and US alphas. If one is willing to assume that US media are sufficiently consistent in their coverage to justify referring to a US media agenda, the same should apply to Canadian media. Whether there is enough inter-newspaper consistency in either country is debatable: there is no line marking an absolute division between enough consistency and not enough consistency. The alphas do seem relatively high, however, especially considering the many variables that intervene between real-world events and published newspaper articles. Those issues that show less consistency (debt and deficit, unemployment) deserve some extra attention in later analyses, perhaps. Overall, however, these tests show that for most issues there is a relatively high degree of inter-newspaper consistency in Canada.

Temporal Trends: Issue Salience and Inter-Newspaper Consistency

There is evidence that consistency in issue coverage is unrelated to newspaper ownership, and that the links between content and region are weak and inconsistent across issues. Consistency might also be expected to change over time, however, based on issue salience. When an issue is in a period of heightened salience, it seems likely that all newspapers will react. When the issue is not especially salient, on the other hand, newspapers may be more likely to react differently to stories on that issue.

Table 3.3 presents more reliability data for Canadian newspaper series, this time divided into three equal intervals. The table presents both Cronbach's alpha and the mean number of articles for each period. If alphas are highest during periods with the highest mean number of articles, this may be an indication that consistency in issue coverage is related to issue salience.

The evidence in Table 3.3 supports this hypothesis. Looking first at the mean number of articles across periods, there are no significantly different means for either debt/deficit or unemployment, based on Tukey's Honestly Significant Differences (HSD) test. It is difficult to glean evidence from either of these issues. For the other six issues, however, the highest mean is significantly different from the other two means. And for five of the six issues –

Table 3.3

Consistency in newspaper coverage over time

		Period		
Issue	Statistic	Wk1 1985 – Wk34 1988	Wk35 1988 – Wk17 1992	Wk18 1992 – Wk52 1995
Prominent issues				
Inflation	Alpha	0.668	**0.678**	0.650
	Mean	2.184	3.482*	2.497
Unemployment	Alpha	0.368	0.320	**0.374**
	Mean	2.689	2.309	3.058
Sensational issues				
AIDS	Alpha	**0.514**	0.392	0.475
	Mean	7.395*	6.052	5.115
Crime	Alpha	0.312	0.323	**0.549**
	Mean	6.032	6.424	9.539*
Environment	Alpha	0.373	**0.551**	0.331
	Mean	3.084*	11.335*	6.440*
Governmental issues				
Debt/deficit	Alpha	0.342	**0.478**	0.194
	Mean	0.689	0.686	0.880
National unity	Alpha	0.661	0.446	**0.735**
	Mean	6.058	12.304*	6.215
Taxes	Alpha	0.087	**0.849**	0.750
	Mean	0.474*	9.937*	2.550*
N		190	191	191

Note: Cells contain Cronbach's alphas and the mean number of articles per week, using weekly data for all Canadian newspapers from 1985 to 1995. Text in bold indicates the highest alpha for each issue. An asterisk indicates that the mean is significantly different (at $p < .05$) from both other means, based on Tukey's HSD test.

AIDS, crime, environment, inflation, and taxes – the greatest alpha value for an issue is during the period with the highest mean number of articles.

These results suggest that inter-newspaper consistency in coverage is greater when issue salience is high. The idea of a single newspaper agenda, then, is likely on stronger ground during periods of heightened issue salience.

Summary and Conclusions

The analyses presented above lead to three conclusions about the media agenda.

First, evidence based on both Canadian and US media time series suggests that there is a good deal of similarity among Canadian newspapers where issue salience is concerned. This finding contrasts starkly with many previous findings and assumptions. It is likely due in part to this study's concentration on simple issue salience rather than on the actual content of newspaper articles. Nevertheless, these above findings indicate that there is considerably more similarity in newspaper agendas in Canada than is generally assumed. Moreover, it indicates that combining the eight newspapers into a single measure will provide an accurate measure of the Canadian newspaper agenda, putting analyses in subsequent chapters on more solid ground.

Second, there is little evidence of regional or ownership-based trends among the newspapers surveyed here. This is in accordance with earlier work. Despite widespread belief that the growth of media magnates has led to more restricted media content, empirical evidence of this trend has been difficult to find.

Finally, there is a relationship between issue salience and consistency in issue coverage. This is an important finding, suggesting that the idea of a Canadian newspaper agenda is on stronger ground when issue salience is high. Moreover, this finding suggests that the potential for media influence may increase when issue salience is high, not only because of increased salience but also because of more consistent coverage across a number of newspapers.

4
The Public Agenda

> The press may, unconsciously, provide a limited and rotating set
> of public issues, around which the political and social system can
> engage in dialogue. In fact, from the point of view of the social
> system, that may be the major "function" of the news media in
> our country. The press does not tell us what to believe, but does
> suggest what we collectively may agree to discuss and perhaps
> act on.
>
> – Donald L. Shaw and Shannon E. Martin (1992, 902-903)

Shaw and Martin's conclusions, suggesting that the media agenda can act as a "social magnet" for groups with otherwise divergent issue concerns, are especially interesting in the Canadian context. Canada is a diverse country, after all, so the need for a social magnet might be especially great. And the potential for this effect seems strong in light of the preceding chapter's evidence of a pan-Canadian media agenda.

We should not assume that Canadian media and public agendas exhibit similar trends and traits, however, especially where national similarities are concerned. The vast bulk of Canadian political debate, after all, is centred around growing regionalism, Quebec separation, and an increasingly fragile Canadian national identity. As with the media agenda, the existence of a pan-Canadian public agenda is not clear. Accordingly, just as the preceding chapter explored the Canadian media agenda, this chapter tests for the existence of a Canadian public agenda.

The chapter begins with a discussion of the methods by which public agendas have been measured, and sources of the "most important problem" (MIP) question are described. The focus then turns to an investigation of Canadian national and regional public agendas. Previous work on Canadian public opinion has identified both similarities and differences. Where issue salience is concerned, however, the evidence here indicates that changes in aggregate public agendas are remarkably similar across Canada.

There is, nevertheless, variation in issue salience across provinces, and explaining this variation is this chapter's final goal. Comparisons of provincial issue saliences include a brief discussion of audience attributes as well as studies into how variations in real-world factors affect public opinion. In spite of a rather cursory analysis, there is a clear link between the perceived salience of issues and their real-world significance across provinces.

Measuring the Public Agenda

Measurement of issue salience for the public is most often based on the "most important problem" question. This question has been asked relatively consistently in the United States and elsewhere (Smith 1980, 1985; Soroka 2001), and reads, with minor variations, as follows: What do you think is the most important issue facing our country today?

Funkhouser's longitudinal public agenda-setting study (1973) is the first to use Gallup's MIP question to measure the public agenda. While Funkhouser uses rank-ordering of issues to represent agendas, however, the open-ended Gallup MIP question has been used repeatedly by other authors to measure the salience of individual issues on the public agenda (e.g., Iyengar and Simon 1993; MacKuen and Coombs 1981; Neuman 1990; Shoemaker et al. 1989; Winter and Eyal 1981; Zucker 1978). In most cases, the proportion of respondents citing a given issue has been used as an indication of that issue's importance on the public agenda.

The MIP question has advantages and disadvantages. Because it is an open-ended question, it does not bias the response. Open-ended questions, however, "reduce the comparability across subjects, and their use invites a certain amount of subjectivity in subsequent coding" (DeGeorge 1981, 220). The MIP question in particular may present some additional difficulties. The use of the word "most," for instance, likely creates even more volatility in an already rather volatile public opinion (Eaton 1989; Wlezien 2001). Moreover, it may be unrealistic to assume that complex public opinions can be accurately measured with a single response, even to an open-ended survey question. MacKuen and Coombs (1981) suggest that the question does not elicit a well-thought-out response, and that the responses are "unaccountably oriented toward the most casual, and superficial, aspects of the public's political consciousness." Nevertheless, they conclude, when its limitations are taken into account, the MIP question does "provide us with an indication of a substantively interesting aspect of public consciousness" (MacKuen and Coombs 1981, 61).

Above and beyond its theoretical strengths and weaknesses, the largest single advantage of the MIP question is that it is one of the very few questions that has been asked relatively consistently by a large number of polling firms for an extended period. This is the often unstated but implicit advantage of the MIP question in past agenda-setting work, and this study is no different. No other opinion question has been asked as frequently as the MIP question, and it is one of the very few questions for which longitudinal analysis of a considerable scale is viable.

Accordingly, the MIP question is used here as the measure of the public agenda. This work is premised, then, on a belief that the MIP question provides a reasonable measure of issue salience – certainly as good a measure as can be expected from one question, and likely the only measure available over a reasonable time period.

Unfortunately, Gallup Canada has not been as consistent with the MIP question as its US counterpart. Question and coding changes have occurred in both countries, but the frequency of the Gallup MIP question is much lower in Canada. This is perhaps one reason why longitudinal agenda-setting research has proliferated in the US but languished in Canada – the availability of public opinion data makes US analyses considerably more convenient. A recent Canadian agenda-setting analysis suggested that a media content analysis could be used in place of a direct measure of the public agenda (Howlett 1997); this conceptual log-jam is presumably partly a function of data availability (see Soroka 1999b).

A major task of the present study, then, is to locate enough MIP questions over time to create a reasonable longitudinal measure of issue salience for the public. Gallup data are used, but the data are combined with surveys from Environics, Decima, Angus Reid, Pollara, and several CBC/*Globe and Mail* polls. The individual surveys and questions are listed in Appendix C. While the wording of questions varies because different polling firms' data are used, it is suggested here that the questions elicit comparable responses (see Appendix C). For months where there is more than one poll, the surveys are merged, and the percentage of responses is calculated from the total sample.

"Canadian" Public Opinion and Agendas

There has been little work on issue salience for the Canadian public, and none comparing issue salience at the provincial level. Previous work does not indicate whether there is considerable provincial variation in issue salience, and cannot indicate whether the use of a Canadian national agenda is problematic. Issue opinions have been analyzed more frequently but results are mixed, indicating a combination of difference and similarity across Canada.

The edited volume *Small Worlds* is one of the more wide-ranging examinations of regional differences in public opinion in Canada. In it, Elkins (1980) examines the importance of regional identities in Canada, while Simeon and Elkins (1980, 31) explore "regional or provincial differences in sense of efficacy, in the degree of citizen's trust in their governments, and in the degree and type of involvement in political matters." Difference is not the overarching theme, however. Simeon and Blake (1980), for instance, find a combination of difference and similarity, marked by over-time convergence, in regional opinion on public policy issues.

Other research supports the dual findings of similarity and difference. Johnston et al.'s investigation (1996) of public opinion surrounding the 1992 constitutional referendum provides evidence of regional differences in opinion, while Fletcher and Howe (1999) find few regional differences in support for the Charter of Rights and Freedoms and courts across regions. Johnston's review (1986) of Canadian public opinion and public policy suggests that regional public opinion is divided on policies within provincial jurisdiction but is similar on federal powers. The fact that several studies deal with Canadian opinion at a national level only is itself a further indication that region does not always play a role in Canadian public opinion. For instance, Nevitte's study (1996) of value change explores themes such as postmodernism, confidence in government, and moral and economic opinion, but makes little mention of regional variation.

In spite of considerable and widely acknowledged differences in public opinion across Canadian regions, then, there is also evidence of substantial similarity. Which will be reflected in measures of issue salience? If there are strong links between media and public agendas, work in Chapter 3 suggests that issue salience should vary little across provinces. Media and public agendas can diverge, however, so public opinion hypotheses based on media data are on shaky ground. The following section tests the existence of national trends in issue salience for the public using provincial results for the MIP question.

Interprovincial Consistency: Exploring Longitudinal Variation

Public opinion data collected for this study are an amalgam of primary data and aggregated results. As a result, separating the national results into provincial samples is not always possible. The Decima data are the most easily accessible at the provincial level, so only these data are used here to compare provincial agendas. While this leads to a reduced number of cases and issues, the analysis should nevertheless offer an adequate picture of provincial differences in issue salience. Moreover, it should point to the validity of a single measure of the Canadian public agenda.

The Decima data enable a comparison of provincial public agendas across five issues: debt/deficit, environment, inflation, national unity, and unemployment. Table 4.1 presents Cronbach's alpha results for each issue, measuring the degree to which changes in issue salience in the ten Canadian provinces are connected. The results show a high degree of interprovincial similarity in issue salience: all alpha coefficients are close to 1. In factor

Table 4.1

Consistency in issue salience across provinces

Issue	Alpha (N)
Debt/deficit	0.950 (24)
Environment	0.952 (24)
Inflation	0.858 (41)
National unity	0.981 (40)
Unemployment	0.965 (41)

Note: Cells contain Cronbach's alphas, using Decima monthly MIP responses, by province, from 1985 to 1995. Sample sizes (*N*) are in parentheses.

analyses (not presented here), all ten provinces load on a single factor for all issues but inflation. Most striking is the extremely high degree of interprovincial similarity for the national unity issue. This is an issue for which there are clearly interprovincial differences in opinion. From 1985 to 1995, however, changes in the salience of this issue were similar across Canada.

The results in Table 4.1 indicate that there is a coherent Canadian public agenda. Interpreting these results, however, should include a consideration of two further issues.

First, some might charge that the positive results are aided by the wording of the MIP question: asking for the "most important problem facing Canada today" might predispose respondents to giving nationally oriented answers. It is possible that answers might reflect what respondents suspect is the greatest national problem, and not the problem that they themselves see as the most important, thereby creating a greater degree of national consensus than actually exists. For instance, Smith (1980, 165) notes that in the Gallup question "the frame of reference is the country at large, and responses inevitably deal with national or even global concerns rather than local or personal problems." Question wording varies across polling firms, however, and Decima, on whose data the results presented here are based, adds the caveat, "in other words, the one that concerns you personally the most." The fact that there is no regional variation in results despite this individually oriented question wording, is likely an indication that the evidence of a Canadian agenda presented here is genuine rather than a product of question design.

Second, we should keep in mind the difference between opinions and salience when considering the evidence of consistency displayed in Table 4.1. There is no question that English and French Canadians feel differently about national unity (see Johnston et al. 1996), and national unity is probably not the only issue for which opinion changes across regions. The evidence presented here, however, indicates that the *salience* of issues tends to be similar across Canada. While Quebeckers and British Columbians may have different opinions, issues are usually salient in both provinces at the same time.

Interprovincial Differences: Exploring Cross-Sectional Variation
Although interprovincial differences in issue salience are small, they do exist. Table 4.2 is a case in point, presenting the average percentage of provincial respondents citing debt or deficit as the most important problem in Decima polls over the survey period. (The provinces' national rankings are noted in parentheses.) These data should be regarded only as very loose estimates of interprovincial difference in issue salience from 1985 to 1995, but the results are telling. While the alpha coefficient in Table 4.1 is very high for debt/deficit, for instance, Table 4.2 shows a large degree of interprovincial variation. Thus, while issue salience tends to rise and fall simultaneously across provinces, the alpha coefficients hide interprovincial differences in the size of public concern. In short, interprovincial similarities are much stronger longitudinally than they are cross-sectionally.

Is it possible to account for cross-sectional variation in issue salience? One hypothesis is that cross-sectional variation is a product of interprovincial differences in audience attributes. This certainly seems the best explanation for differences in the salience of the national unity issue, for instance, based on the hypothesis that salience of national unity issues is related to the size of a province's francophone population.

Table 4.3 tests this hypothesis, contrasting interprovincial differences in salience with the percentage of the population whose mother tongue is French. Two correlation coefficients are noted in the final row: Pearson's *r* is calculated using the actual values in the first and second columns, and

Table 4.2

Provincial issue salience: debt/deficit

Province	Average % respondents
Newfoundland	3.440 (10)
Prince Edward Island	6.416 (8)
Nova Scotia	7.704 (6)
New Brunswick	6.263 (9)
Quebec	7.351 (7)
Ontario	7.832 (5)
Manitoba	10.803 (4)
Saskatchewan	14.400 (2)
Alberta	16.766 (1)
British Columbia	14.103 (3)

Note: N = 24. Cells contain average % respondents, using Decima monthly MIP responses, by province, from 1985 to 1995. Provincial rankings are in parentheses.

Table 4.3

Provincial issue salience and audience attributes: national unity

Province	Average % respondents[a]		Francophone population (%)[b]	
Newfoundland	4.647	(9)	0.4	(10)
Prince Edward Island	5.174	(7)	4.2	(5)
Nova Scotia	5.171	(8)	3.9	(6)
New Brunswick	7.722	(2)	32.9	(2)
Quebec	9.276	(1)	80.9	(1)
Ontario	5.794	(6)	4.5	(3)
Manitoba	7.314	(3)	4.3	(4)
Saskatchewan	4.613	(10)	2.0	(7)
Alberta	6.049	(5)	2.0	(7)
British Columbia	6.836	(4)	1.4	(9)
Pearson's *r*		0.813**		
Spearman's rho		0.657*		

Notes: N = 40.
[a] Cells contain average % respondents, using Decima monthly MIP responses, by province, from 1985 to 1995. Provincial rankings are in parentheses.
[b] Data from Statistics Canada, 1996 Census, Census Data Analyser at the University of Toronto.
* $p < .05$, ** $p < .01$, *** $p < .001$

Spearman's rho is a measure of correlation between provincial rankings, which are noted in parentheses in each column. Both correlation coefficients are high and statistically significant, pointing to a relationship between aggregate concern about national unity and provincial francophone population.

Francophone population is only one of several variables that may be correlated with concern about national unity. The comparatively high concern in the West, for instance, is attributable to other factors. Nevertheless, the results in Table 4.3 point to the relationship between language and national unity salience. They also indicate the relationship between issue salience and audience attributes, and consequently point to the important contributions that more complex individual-level analysis can make to models of agenda-setting.

Another hypothesis is that interprovincial differences in issue salience are related to differences in real-world factors. Tables 4.4 and 4.5 go some way towards testing – and validating – this hypothesis. Table 4.4 compares the average provincial salience of inflation with provincial changes in the consumer price index (CPI), while Table 4.5 compares the average provincial salience of unemployment with the average provincial unemployment rates from 1985 to 1995. In both cases, provinces that score high on the real-world measure also score high on average issue salience, as reflected by the relatively high Pearson's *r* and Spearman's rho coefficients. This is more

Table 4.4

Provincial issue salience and real-world indicators: inflation

Province	Average % respondents[a]		CPI change from 1985 to1995[b]	
Newfoundland	2.837	(8)	30.3	(10)
Prince Edward Island	2.134	(10)	33.1	(8)
Nova Scotia	3.852	(4)	33.3	(7)
New Brunswick	3.091	(6)	32.6	(9)
Quebec	2.983	(7)	35.5	(6)
Ontario	4.101	(2)	38.7	(3)
Manitoba	3.763	(3)	39.7	(2)
Saskatchewan	4.752	(1)	38.5	(4)
Alberta	3.516	(5)	36.0	(5)
British Columbia	2.208	(9)	40.2	(1)
Pearson's *r*			0.328	
Spearman's rho			0.382	

Notes: N = 41.
[a] Cells contain average % respondents, using Decima monthly MIP responses, by province, from 1985 to 1995. Provincial rankings are in parentheses.
[b] Data from Statistics Canada, Selected Economic Indicators – Provinces, CANSIM matrices 6968-6977.
* $p < .05$, ** $p < .01$, *** $p < .001$

Table 4.5

Provincial issue salience and real-world indicators: unemployment

Province	Average % respondents[a]		Average unemployment rate (1985-95)[b]	
Newfoundland	49.917	(1)	18.64	(1)
Prince Edward Island	33.691	(3)	15.30	(2)
Nova Scotia	34.481	(2)	12.30	(4)
New Brunswick	31.808	(4)	12.87	(3)
Quebec	31.350	(5)	11.24	(5)
Ontario	22.177	(7)	7.91	(9)
Manitoba	22.800	(6)	8.26	(8)
Saskatchewan	20.208	(10)	7.52	(10)
Alberta	21.408	(9)	8.74	(7)
British Columbia	21.988	(8)	10.47	(6)
Pearson's *r*			0.946***	
Spearman's rho			0.867**	

Notes: N = 41.
[a] Cells contain average % respondents, using Decima monthly MIP responses, by province, from 1985 to 1995. Provincial rankings are in parentheses.
[b] Data from Statistics Canada, Selected Economic Indicators – Provinces, CANSIM matrices 6968-6977.
* $p < .05$, ** $p < .01$, *** $p < .001$

true for unemployment than for inflation, admittedly. British Columbians appear to have remained comparatively unconcerned about inflation in the face of high inflation. Removing BC from the analysis, however, leads to significant coefficients for both Pearson's r and Spearman's rho. These results echo predictions made in Chapter 2 and foreshadow evidence found in Chapter 6: particularly for prominent issues, issue salience is directly connected to real-world indicators of issue severity.

Summary and Conclusions

Previous work on Canadian public opinion tends to emphasize a combination of similarity and difference, and this study follows suit. In the first analyses, comparing provincial agendas indicates considerable similarity in changes in issue salience across provinces; despite widely acknowledged regional differences in issue opinions, the salience of issues tends to rise and fall at the same time across the country. Thus, there is good reason to speak of a Canadian public agenda: when an issue is rising in importance in the West, the East is experiencing a similar trend.

The magnitude of attention across regions is often quite different, however, as this chapter has also demonstrated. The longitudinal similarity initially explored above appears to hide a certain degree of cross-sectional difference, and a comparison of average salience scores across provinces reveals patterns to this difference related to regional variation in audience attributes and real-world conditions. National unity provides an example of the relationship between audience attributes and issue salience: while trends in the salience of national unity are similar across provinces, the issue is consistently more salient in regions with larger francophone populations. Inflation and unemployment, on the other hand, demonstrate a link between real-world conditions and issue salience.

Figure 4.1 offers a useful demonstration of the trends described above. It illustrates the salience of unemployment over time, using Decima data, for the two provinces with the highest and the two provinces with the lowest average unemployment rates from 1985 to 1995. (Prince Edward Island is excluded because it has so few cases.) Results for the provinces clearly follow the same path, declining until 1990 and then rising steadily until 1995. Issue salience for provinces with high unemployment, however, is always higher than for provinces with low unemployment. Longitudinal similarities are strong, as indicated in the Cronbach's alpha score in Table 4.1, but there are considerable cross-sectional differences; these are clearly linked with regional differences in real-world conditions.

Figure 4.1

Salience of the unemployment issue, by province

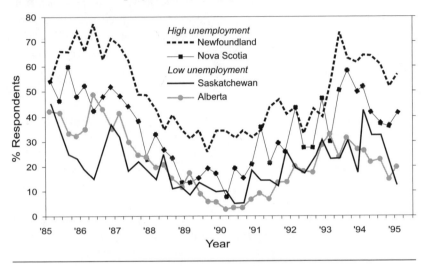

This chapter indicates that while we can use a national longitudinal measure of public salience, we should not ignore the fact that there are important cross-sectional – or cross-regional – differences. This finding should not adversely affect tests in subsequent chapters that use a national measure, although there is a slight possibility that evidence of causal effects will be more difficult to find for issues in which provincial public opinion differs in both level and variance. In these cases, province-level agenda-setting analysis might be more likely to discover strong effects. Tests in succeeding chapters indicate that this is likely not a problem for the cases surveyed here, however. Rather, the results described in this chapter remind us that Canadian public opinion does indeed reflect a combination of similarity and difference, and point to the importance of further cross-sectional work in agenda-setting modelling.

5
The Policy Agenda

It would be interesting to attempt to relate policy decisions during
the sixties – for example, legislation and fund allocation – to the
trends in events and media attention.

— G. Ray Funkhouser (1973, 75)

Although his own work deals with public opinion and media content,
Funkhouser was among the first agenda-setting researchers to recognize the
value of connecting public- and policy-oriented agenda-setting analyses.
Twenty years passed before an explicit attempt was made to do so, however,
and even then analyses made only half-hearted efforts to include adequate
measures of media, public, *and* policy agendas. This study represents one of
the first efforts to respond to Funkhouser's assertion. Doing so requires policy
agenda measures, however, and specifying the policy agenda is a difficult
task, especially outside the United States.

This chapter examines the potentials and pitfalls in measuring the Canadian policy agenda. In general, it shows that measuring the Canadian policy
agenda is decidedly more difficult than measuring the public or media agendas. In the case of the latter, measurement possibilities are limited, based on
the nature of the agendas themselves, data availability, and the relatively
consistent choices made in past agenda-setting work.

The same cannot be said for the policy agenda. There is a considerable
body of literature dealing with it, but the measures used vary widely.
Moreover, the vast majority of previous empirical policy agenda-setting work
deals with the US, and examples do not always translate well into other
political systems. The US system of government, based on a combination of
divided jurisdiction and openness, allows for a wide range of reasonably
accurate empirical measures of policy attention. Roll calls, legislative initiatives, committee meetings, and press releases are just some of the congressional activities that are accurately recorded and easily accessible. In the

Canadian parliamentary system, on the other hand, the most easily available sources are records of discussions in the House of Commons and Senate *(Hansard)*, where little actual decision making takes place. Most important policy discussions occur unrecorded in bureaucratic venues or cabinet meetings. This is not to say that policy measures in Canada are impossible, but they are certainly more limited.

This chapter deals with this difficulty by considering the wide range of policy agenda measures used in US studies. Each measure is introduced in turn, and its applicability to the Canadian system is discussed. As in preceding chapters, various agenda measures are compared and contrasted. Unlike the media and public agendas, however, identifying a single policy agenda measure is not the objective here. Rather, the aim of this chapter is to investigate different ways in which the policy agenda can be measured, examine the reliability of and relationships between these measures, and propose methods of including most of them in agenda-setting models used in subsequent analyses.

The chapter begins with a discussion of government spending, the only policy measure discussed here that is not included in forthcoming agenda-setting models. It then discusses three policy measures that can be adapted to monthly time series analysis: committee activities, Throne Speech content, and legislation. Each measure is introduced and some preliminary tests are conducted; evidence shows that each responds in varying degrees to the trends evident in media and public series. Next, each is compared with what is used as the primary monthly measure of the policy agenda – a content analysis of Question Period discussions in *Hansard*. The degree to which other measures are reflected in the Question Period time series is tested. The chapter finishes with a conceptual discussion of policy agenda measures and a proposal for representing the policy agenda in succeeding chapters.

Government Spending

Government spending is the most obvious and easily accessible empirical measure of the policy agenda. Issue-specific spending is used in a number of US agenda-setting studies (e.g., Baumgartner and Jones 1993; Hall and Jones 1997; Rogers et al. 1991). In Canada, studies of political business cycles and partisanship effects use overall spending as a measure of ideological or political agendas (e.g., Cameron 1986; Simeon and Miller 1980; Petry 1995; Petry et al. 1999; Blais et al. 1996).

Government spending presents a number of difficulties, however. First and foremost is the fact that spending estimates are yearly, making any longitudinal research at a higher frequency difficult. It is possible to obtain some spending figures at monthly intervals, but these probably do not reflect changes in issue salience. It is also possible to extrapolate annual data into monthly data (as in Rogers et al. 1991), but this creates a highly autocorrelated series with jumps that reflect budgetary constraints rather than actual changes in issue salience for policymakers. For analyses such as this one, which covers a decade in monthly intervals, spending data are far from ideal.

Moreover, it is possible that incremental changes in yearly spending data are a poor indication of changes in issue salience. Wildavsky (1964) presents what are perhaps the best-known hypotheses on "incrementalism" in budgetary processes – the fact that one year's budget is based almost entirely on the previous year's. If this is true, we should expect to see very little change in spending even when there are dramatic changes in issue salience. The incremental nature of spending data has been recognized by agenda-setting theorists (e.g., Pritchard and Berkowitz 1993). Furthermore, Savoie's review (1990, 336) of spending in Canada partly supports Wildavsky's hypothesis: "As elsewhere, an important determining factor in the size of the main estimates tabled by the federal government is the previous year's main estimates."

Savoie (1990, 36) continues: "In Canada, however, federal ministers and officials have demonstrated a knack to start new programs quickly." Thus, while Canadian federal budgets typically change incrementally, it is possible that changes in salience will be reflected in government spending. In fact, recent research in the US suggests that measures of government spending can show considerably more variation than incrementalist theories suggest (Jones et al. 1997).

Nevertheless, the potential of spending data to reflect issue salience may be restricted to long-term studies. Jones et al. (1997), after all, analyzed the entire postwar era. An additional and perhaps more significant caveat is that spending data will likely be useful only when the time period analyzed includes major shifts in the policy agenda. Year-to-year budgetary variations may normally be small, unreflective of comparatively minor changes in policy and consequently unresponsive to changes in the media and public agendas. It follows that, for periods during which an issue experiences only minor changes in salience, spending will not reflect such changes. Periods of major agenda change, however, are more likely to be reflected in government spending.

What do government spending data tell us about the issues investigated here? Figure 5.1 illustrates federal government spending figures from 1985 to 1995 for those issues for which spending data are readily available. All amounts are calculated as a proportion of both total government spending and total government spending excluding debt and transfer payments. The second calculation is included in case excluding these forms of "mandatory" spending (Jones et al. 1997) drastically alters the over-time dynamics; results show that it does not. Details of all the government spending measures are included in Appendix D.

Figure 5.1

Federal government spending, by issue

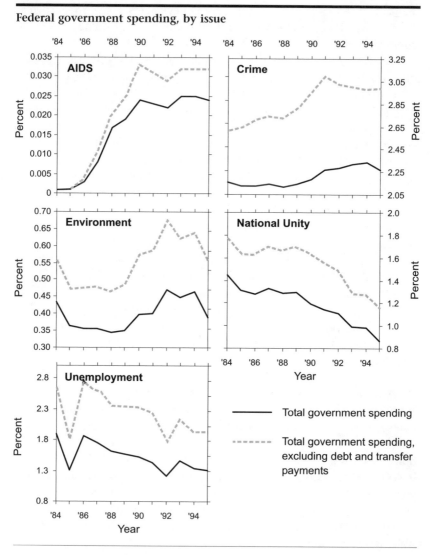

Figure 5.1 indicates that it is possible for government spending to reflect short-term changes in issue salience. Major changes in AIDS spending from 1987 to 1989, for instance, reflect the appearance of that issue on the federal agenda. Similarly, increases in environmental spending from 1990 to 1992 are the product of government attention to environmental issues from 1989 to 1991, and two jumps in unemployment spending (spending on job creation and training programs, not unemployment insurance) in 1986 and

1993 also reflect major policy change. Finally, increased crime spending appears to match the expected increase in crime salience over this period. Figure 5.1 shows, however, that national unity spending decreases over the survey period and does not show the jumps in 1988 and 1992 that we might have expected. This may be due to the difficulty in measuring national unity expenditures, or it might be that concern for these issues was simply not reflected in spending priorities.

In four out of five cases, then, there is an apparent connection between spending priorities and our expectations regarding short-term changes in issue salience. Admittedly, the apparent value of using spending data is enhanced somewhat by the issues selected for analysis, issues that showed dramatic changes in salience during the survey period. Nevertheless, Figure 5.1 suggests the potential for spending data in yearly analyses, in line with recent work in the US.

Despite their potential for yearly analysis, however, spending data are an inadequate higher-frequency measure of the policy agenda, and are therefore not used in the agenda-setting modelling in Chapters 6 and 7. The monthly agenda-setting work that follows relies on measures that exhibit greater change at shorter intervals.

Committees

Congressional hearings have been used as a measure of the US policy agenda, most comprehensively by Baumgartner and Jones (1993) but also by Bartels (1996), Sharp (1994), and Hall and Jones (1997). Hearings are drawn from the Congressional Information Service (CIS) Abstracts, or from the Federal News Service and *Congressional Record,* and the number of subject-specific hearings in a given period is taken as an indication of issue salience.

It is not clear that committees will indicate issue salience for policymakers in Canada, however. In the US, committees are a fundamental part of the policy process; they are, in many cases, the single most important forum for policy discussion. Canadian House and Senate committees, on the other hand, play a much smaller role. The secondary role of committees is reflected in the fact that before the 1980s – excluding meetings to review departmental estimates – standing committees had the authority to meet only on receipt of an order of reference from the House. Moreover, a bill has already been discussed in caucus before it arrives in a House committee, and government members are expected to support it in committee discussions (Matheson 1976). As a result, committees have had little input in policy debates and have rarely been an effective check on cabinet power. Even the most important committees are regarded as ineffectual and are poorly attended (March 1974, 112-13).

Many expected this to change in the mid-1980s, following recommendations by the Lefebvre and McGrath Committees. Standing committees were given the power to hire staff and to decide when they would meet and what they would discuss – a clear step towards increased committee power. Subsequent reviews, however, including the 1993 Report of the Liaison Committee on Committee Effectiveness, indicate that this has not been the case (Franks 1987; Savoie 1990, 1999). Rather, stringent partisanship and a concentration of power in the cabinet – and particularly the prime minister – continue to undermine the effectiveness of House committees: "Even committee chairs are not protected from an angry leader. Members sit in both of these positions at the discretion of the prime minister, and can be removed if their actions displease their leader. In the 35th Parliament, for instance, voting against his government's budget cost Justice Committee Chair Warren Allmand his position" (Docherty 1997, 23). Assessments of Canadian parliamentary committees are in agreement: marred by a collection of reputational, procedural, and parliamentary system–related problems, most committees' impact on policies has been trivial.

The fact that Canadian committees do not play an important role in the policy process appears to preclude the possibility that they could serve as a useful indicator of the policy agenda. Howlett's data (1997) may indicate otherwise, however. His Canadian agenda-setting analysis found weak correlations between issue mentions in committee reports and mentions in Canadian newspapers and periodicals, indicating that, in spite of their minor policymaking role, committees may serve as an indication of changing issue salience. Further evidence that committee data can indicate changing salience is offered in Tables 5.1 and 5.2.

Table 5.1 tracks hours in committee meetings over the survey period for those issues for which there are related committees. The lack of a Canadian version of the CIS makes tracking committee meetings extremely difficult; the data here are based on the Annual Report of the Committees and Legislative Services Directorate. Data are available only by fiscal year, and so are presented in that format. Yearly data are reported in both real numbers and as a proportion of the total to control for yearly changes in the use of committees, and cells with values of zero are left blank to emphasize the possibility of missing data. Because committee meeting data are coded by committee name and not by the actual content of meetings, it is likely that some issue-related meetings are missing. The fact that there are no data for inflation, for instance, is an indication of the problems in coding committee meetings by committee title. As a result, these data should be regarded as only a preliminary analysis; a more comprehensive and reliable dataset would entail coding the minutes of meetings by all committees.

Table 5.2 tracks similar data for committee reports tabled in the House. The data are taken from an exhaustive list of committee reports, coded by title and aggregated by fiscal year to facilitate comparison with the committee meeting data.

Table 5.1

Parliamentary committee meetings, by fiscal year

				Issue			
Fiscal year	AIDS	Crime	Debt/deficit	Environment	National unity	Taxes	Unemployment
86-87	–	–	–	82.52 / 3%	194.44 / 7.1%	–	–
87-88	–	–	–	43.75 / 1.3%	167.65 / 5%	–	–
88-89	–	–	–	41.97 / 4.5%	26.31 / 2.8%	–	–
89-90	–	–	–	140.52 / 8.3%	32.25 / 1.9%	–	–
90-91	–	68.4 / 4.7%	10.1 / 0.7%	158.9 / 10.8%	304.7 / 20.7%	–	–
91-92	–	5.2 / 0.4%	–	97.3 / 6.9%	423.8 / 30.1%	23.7 / 1.7%	–
92-93	–	25.6 / 1.9%	–	56.6 / 4.1%	14.9 / 1.1%	5.6 / 0.4%	–
93-94	–	–	–	44.3 / 5.8%	30.4 / 4%	–	–
94-95	14.9 / 0.5%	–	–	218.3 / 7.9%	173.6 / 6.2%	–	–
95-96	27.6 / 1.8%	–	–	149 / 9.5%	101.3 / 6.5%	–	–

Note: Cells contain the number of related hours in committee, followed by the percent of total number of hours in all committees.

Table 5.2

Parliamentary committee reports, by fiscal year

Fiscal year	Issue						
	AIDS	Crime	Debt/deficit	Environment	National unity	Taxes	Unemployment
86-87	1 / 9.1%	1 / 9.1%	–	–	–	–	2 / 18.2%
87-88	–	–	–	1 / 11.1%	3 / 33.3%	–	–
88-89	–	–	–	–	–	–	1 / 33.3%
89-90	–	–	–	1 / 25.0%	1 / 25.0%	–	–
90-91	–	2 / 20.0%	1 / 10.0%	4 / 40.0%	1 / 10.0%	–	–
91-92	–	10 / 50.0%	2 / 10.0%	4 / 20.0%	2 / 10.0%	–	–
92-93	–	9 / 32.1%	1 / 3.6%	9 / 32.1%	5 / 17.9%	23.7 / 1.7%	–
93-94	1 / 8.3%	5 / 41.7%	1 / 8.3%	2 / 16.7%	1 / 8.3%	5.6 / 0.4%	–
94-95	–	4 / 23.5%	1 / 5.9%	6 / 35.3%	–	–	1 / 8.3%
95-96	1 / 8.3%	4 / 33.3%	–	5 / 41.7%	–	–	2 / 11.8%

Note: Cells contain the number of related committee reports, followed by the percent of total number of committee reports.

Tables 5.1 and 5.2 show that trends in committee meetings and reports are loosely correlated with the trends in salience that the issue histories in Chapter 2 lead us to expect. For instance, environmental reports and meetings increased from 1989 to 1991, in line with what we know about government policy discussion and development during this period. National unity meetings also increased from 1990 to 1992 – the period surrounding the Charlottetown Accord discussions – and crime and debt/deficit reports rose in the early 1990s. Unemployment and AIDS committee meeting data do not seem to follow the expected trends, probably because of missing data – both topics are often addressed in committees with titles that do not reflect their issue content – but committee reports are more telling. Unemployment reports surfaced during periods of policy change, and AIDS reports signalled the beginning of government interest and the results of regular government monitoring of AIDS in the mid-1990s.

Thus, trends in committee data provide useful anecdotal evidence in tracing government attention to issues, although using meeting data as a reliable empirical measure would require more readily available data and more ambitious coding. Reports, on the other hand, are easily and accurately recorded. The fact that most committees play a very minor role in policy discussions limits the degree to which one wants to rely on committee data alone. It is possible, however, that committee reports might affect discussion elsewhere; this is tested later in this chapter.

Press Releases, Statements, and Speeches

Content analyses of US presidential speeches have been used as indications of the presidential agenda. Both Gonzenbach (1996) and Andrade and Young (1996), for instance, base their measures of presidential attention to drugs on an analysis of the *Public Papers of the Presidents of the United States*. The latter authors, in fact, suggest that speech content is a better indication of the presidential agenda than legislation-based measures, since there is a wide range of issues that are not necessarily translated into legislation (Andrade and Young 1996, 592; see also Bartels 1996).

The Canadian executive plays a very different role from the White House. In a system of divided government, a president is obliged to rely on speeches and press releases as a principal means of publicizing executive preferences and initiatives. The Canadian prime minister and cabinet, on the other hand, sit in the House and have their hands directly on the policymaking reins in all fields. As a result, the Prime Minister's Office (PMO) and Privy Council Office (PCO) do not often use speeches and press releases to publicize executive policy proposals. The government's initiatives are discussed in caucus and cabinet, and then announced by the appropriate minister through the appropriate ministry. PMO press releases tend to be dominated by statements regarding retirements, deaths, and visiting dignitaries; the only policy discussion found in PMO press releases with any frequency deals with foreign policy. Neither these nor ministries' press releases are reliably or consistently collected, nor is it clear that they cover all relevant policy proposals. Many proposals are simply announced in the House.

The Throne Speech may, on the other hand, prove to be a valuable policy agenda measure. Certainly, the State of the Union address has been widely used in US studies. There are rarely clear policy statements in the address – content tends to be more symbolic than substantive (Hinckley 1990) – but symbols play a significant role in political discourse, so a lack of specific policy statements need not take away from the address's value as a declaration of policy priorities (Cohen 1999, 34-37). There is a considerable body of literature based on this premise, which has been widely used in studies of presidential politics (e.g., Hargrove and Nelson 1984; Kessel 1974; Light 1993; Moen 1990; Walcott and Hult 1995). Furthermore, the address's significance has been shown both in interviews with White House staffers (Kingdon 1995; Light 1999) and in agenda-setting studies linking the address with policy priorities, public opinion, and media content (Cohen 1995, 1999; Gilberg et al. 1980; Hill 1998; Miller and Wanta 1996; Wanta 1997; Wanta et al. 1989). The address is a well-planned and calculated statement, and a content analysis provides a valuable indication of presidential priorities.

While the Throne Speech is the Canadian equivalent of the State of the Union address, it has received very little attention from Canadian public policy analysts. This can be attributed only partly to differences between the State of the Union address and the Throne Speech. Because the latter does not take place at regular intervals, for instance, it is not possible to create a yearly time series, as it is with the former. The Throne Speech also seems to show more variance in length and structure than the State of the Union address. These problems can be overcome, however, and the Throne Speech can be used as an indication – albeit an inconsistent one longitudinally – of the government's policy priorities.

Table 5.3 presents a content analysis of the six Throne Speeches given from 1985 to 1995. The content of each speech is taken directly from *Hansard*. Each column line is coded for a single issue, and the number of issue-related lines are divided by the total number of lines to provide the percentage of each Throne Speech dealing with various issues. Not all issues are presented in Table 5.3. The eight issues of special interest are listed first, followed by several other issues that figure prominently in the six speeches. "General" refers to symbolic comments about Canada that have no particular issue content, and all remaining issues are lumped together in a single category.

The Throne Speech for the first session of the Thirty-fourth Parliament (34.1) is a peculiar case. This session was convened briefly in late 1988 to pass the Free Trade Agreement (FTA), so the speech dealt only with free trade and general issues. (The second session began when Parliament re-

Table 5.3

Issue emphasis in Throne Speeches

Parliamentary session

Issue	33.1	33.2	34.1	34.2	34.3	35.1
AIDS	0.00	0.00	0.00	**0.33**	0.00	0.00
Crime	**6.42**	3.58	0.00	2.95	0.39	4.14
Debt/deficit	2.20	1.66	0.00	**7.69**	1.56	4.14
Environment	0.00	2.81	0.00	**15.88**	0.00	0.00
Inflation	0.00	0.26	0.00	0.00	**1.17**	0.00
National unity	11.38	8.94	0.00	11.62	**20.31**	6.05
Taxes	1.47	2.43	0.00	**2.95**	0.00	2.23
Unemployment	4.04	2.17	0.00	**8.84**	1.56	8.28
Other economic	**17.61**	10.34	0.00	12.27	6.90	3.82
Foreign affairs/ defence	**26.79**	11.88	0.00	7.69	3.39	3.18
Free trade/ international trade	0.00	3.70	**49.21**	4.75	7.42	3.82
General	4.77	11.11	50.79	7.69	16.67	14.65
Other	25.32	40.87	0.00	17.51	40.63	49.68

Note: Cells contain the percent of lines in each Throne Speech. Text in bold indicates highest value for each issue.

convened four months later.) Accordingly, this speech offers no information about the issues of primary interest in this study. It is, however, illustrative of hypotheses on issue competition (see, for instance, Hertog et al. 1994; Hilgartner and Bosk 1988; Iyengar and Simon 1993, 376; Zhu 1992) and "killer issues" (Brosius and Kepplinger 1995). These hypotheses suggest that issues compete for limited agenda space, a dynamic especially evident here, as all other issues disappeared from the Throne Speech when the FTA was extremely salient. Moreover, this speech also indicates a clear relationship between Throne Speech content and policy priorities.

Other Throne Speeches do not show the same degree of single-mindedness. If Throne Speeches are accurate statements of a government's priorities, however, issue salience trends found in other policy series should be reflected in the content analyses. Evidence in Table 5.3 shows that this is sometimes the case. The salience of national unity, environment, and debt/deficit in the Throne Speech, for instance, is linked with the salience trends observed in other media, public, and policy measures. National unity content rose during the period of the Charlottetown Accord; environmental issues rose before major initiatives from 1989 to 1991; debt/deficit surfaced before the 1989 budget that first put this issue on the agenda.

The picture is less clear for other issues. A rise in AIDS content precedes a rise in AIDS expenditures in 1989, but there were significant rises in AIDS expenditures from 1986 to 1988 that receive no mention. Crime, inflation, and unemployment mentions also reflect only some of the expected salience dynamics. This may be due in part to the timing of Throne Speeches. The speech is likely an accurate indicator of the government's agenda at the time, but issue salience can change dramatically in the intervals between Throne Speeches. This seriously reduces the potential for Throne Speech content to serve as a functional policy agenda time series, at least on its own. In conjunction with other measures, however, Throne Speech content may prove useful.

Legislation and Legislative Initiatives

Perhaps the clearest indication of policymakers' priorities is policy itself. Legislation is easily collected, and is a widely used measure of the US policy agenda. Baumgartner and Jones' dataset (1993) constitutes the most comprehensive collection of this information, but authors such as Page and Shapiro (1983) have also relied on public policy as an agenda measure. The measure is also easily translated into the Canadian context (see Petry 1999): a variety of sources can be used to record the bills introduced in each session, as well as the days on which the bill was discussed in the House and the Senate.

There are, however, a few methodological issues in recording legislative initiatives. Finished legislation is the clearest indicator of a government's policy priorities, in that it represents those issues important enough to have motivated bill introduction, debate, possible committee discussion, and a vote. By excluding bills that do not survive the policy process, however, we may be missing important information about the policy agenda, which should include all issues that receive attention. Accordingly, a legislation-based measure should likely include all bills that are introduced. This logic is advanced by a number of authors who have suggested using bill introductions as a measure of issue salience in the US Congress (e.g., Wilkerson et al. 1999).

Another issue pertinent to the Canadian context is whether both government and private member's (PM) bills should be used. The former are generally discussed in the governing party's caucus and cabinet, and forwarded by the appropriate minister. They are always debated and almost always passed (since most Canadian governments have a majority in the House). PM bills, on the other hand, are limited in that they cannot be "money" bills, and may never be debated or voted on. The time given to PM bills is limited, so a number of bills are chosen randomly for debate and only a minority of these is selected for a vote. The end result of this process is that PM bills tend to be taken less seriously, are often symbolic in nature, and are very rarely passed.

If both government and PM bills are to be used as indications of the policy agenda, they should probably be included separately. This is the case in Table 5.4, where the number of bills is recorded by fiscal year. Cells include the total number of bills, followed by a division into the number of government and the number of PM bills. The trends in salience evident with other measures are also evident for crime, debt/deficit, and environment. No trends are evident for other issues. The fact that salience trends here are different from elsewhere should not be taken as an indication that the measure is flawed, however; we should not expect all policy series to follow exactly the same movements over time. In fact, the same applies to previous measures: government spending, committee activities, Throne Speeches, and legislative initiatives might each be viewed as individual policy agendas, following paths that can be closely or loosely connected.

Parliamentary Debate

Content analyses of the *Debates of the House of Commons (Hansard)* have informed empirical agenda-setting and other studies in Canada (i.e., Howlett 1997, 1998; Soroka 1999a, 2002a; Tremblay 1998; Crimmins and Nesbitt-Larking 1996), and have been used in various guises in studies of other parliamentary systems (e.g., Breuning 1994; Diskin and Galnoor 1990). The most similar US measure is congressional floor speeches, which have seen limited use (e.g., Bartels 1996). In Canada, however, parliamentary debate has the distinct advantage of being better recorded and more easily accessible than any other policy agenda source, and is the only measure that allows for meaningful measurements on a monthly basis.

Accordingly, this research includes a content analysis of House debates on each issue from 1985 to 1995, and uses this as the primary measure of the policy agenda. Whereas Howlett (1997, 1998) and Soroka (1999a) use the index to identify relevant statements anywhere in *Hansard*, however, the current database was created by manually paging through *Hansard* and recording not only the number of mentions but also the size of each mention, in column centimetres.[1] This was done in large part because of problems with the *Hansard* index, which was found not to be an accurate measure of what is actually in *Hansard*. For the most part, index citations are accurate, but there are numerous obvious and sizable issue mentions in *Hansard* not included in the index. The measure used here includes these mentions,

---

[1] The font and column size change very slightly between the 33rd, 34th, and 35th sessions. To make up for this discrepancy, the time series were adjusted in the following manner: (1) A random sample of 10 cm sections was selected from each session; (2) the words in each 10 cm section were counted; (3) using the average number of words in a 10 cm section for the 33rd, 34th, and 35th Parliaments, a weight was created to adjust the measurements so that they were directly comparable.

Table 5.4

Parliamentary bills, by fiscal year

Fiscal year	Issue						
	AIDS	Crime	Debt/deficit	Environment	National unity	Taxes	Unemployment
84-85	–	9 (1/8)	–	2 (1/1)	2 (0/2)	6 (6/0)	1 (0/1)
85-86	–	16 (6/10)	–	3 (0/3)	1 (0/1)	8 (8/0)	1 (1/0)
86-87	–	18 (5/13)	–	2 (1/1)	3 (0/3)	7 (7/0)	1 (1/0)
87-88	–	10 (5/5)	–	1 (1/0)	3 (2/1)	6 (6/0)	4 (3/1)
88-89	–	10 (3/7)	–	2 (1/1)	1 (1/0)	2 (2/0)	1 (1/0)
89-90	–	28 (5/23)	1 (1/0)	5 (1/4)	4 (3/1)	6 (6/0)	1 (1/0)
90-91	–	10 (1/9)	–	6 (1/5)	–	3 (1/2)	–
91-92	–	33 (7/26)	1 (1/0)	8 (5/3)	1 (0/1)	9 (2/7)	1 (0/1)
92-93	–	27 (5/22)	2 (2/0)	2 (1/1)	2 (1/1)	10 (5/5)	2 (/2)
93-94	–	22 (3/19)	1 (1/0)	–	–	10 (6/4)	5 (0/5)
94-95	–	24 (6/18)	–	4 (3/1)	2 (1/1)	11 (4/7)	2 (1/1)
95-96	–	16 (3/13)	–	2 (2/0)	1 (1/0)	6 (4/2)	3 (2/1)

Note: Cells contain the total number of bills, divided into government and private member's bills in parentheses.

and has the additional advantage of including counts of column centimetres, which offer an indication of issue mention length and so allow for a more nuanced and accurate time series.

Another difference between this and previous *Hansard* measures is that this measure uses only Question Period. Because independent measures are collected for committee reports and bill discussions, most other discussion periods in the House have already been covered. Thus, an analysis of Question Period alone provides a unique opportunity to examine the relationship between this discussion and other policymaking arenas. Moreover, Question Period is by far the most flexible part of House business. Especially flexible, in fact, since, while the British system requires that some questions be tabled in advance, questions in the Canadian system can be entirely spontaneous. As a result, Question Period is the part of parliamentary discussion most susceptible to media influence: "Question period is a freewheeling affair, with tremendous spontaneity and vitality. The main topics are often those on the front pages of the major newspapers, or ones raised on national television news the previous evening" (Franks 1987, 146).

Question Period is probably also the part of the policy process most likely to influence the media and public agendas: parliamentarians, journalists, and the public alike see it as the forum for heated debate and controversy about the most current issues (Taras 1990). When searching for inter-agenda effects, Question Period seems to offer the most potential.

In fact, the flexibility and significance of Question Period is such that other policy measures might be reflected in a Question Period time series. Committee reports or legislative initiatives, for instance, might show up consistently enough that a Question Period content analysis is all that is required to adequately represent the policy agenda. This hypothesis is tested in Table 5.5.

The table presents the results of the following regression model, estimated by ordinary least squares (OLS):

$$Hansard_t = \alpha + \sum_{k=1}^{K} \beta_{1(k)} Hansard_{t-k} + \beta_2 Committees_t + \beta_3 PMBills_t \qquad (5.1)$$
$$+ \beta_4 GVBills_t + \beta_5 THSpeech_t + \beta_6 Sit_t + \varepsilon_t$$

where *Hansard* is the number of issue-related column centimetres in Question Period, *Committees* is the number of committee reports presented in the House, *PMBills* is the number of private member's bill discussions (first, second, or third) in the House, *GVBills* is the number of government bill discussions in the House, and *THSpeech* is the percentage of the Throne Speech dealing with the issue (equal to zero in months when there is no Throne Speech). Equation 5.1 is in fact an autoregressive distributed lag (ADL) model; ADL models are described in Appendix A. In the meantime, suffice it to say

Table 5.5

Modelling Question Period

Dependent variable: $Hansard_t$

Independent variables	AIDS β	SE(β)	Crime β	SE(β)	Debt/deficit β	SE(β)	Environment β	SE(β)
Constant	-1.551	(3.757)	-31.854*	(13.664)	-3.343	(8.378)	-39.774	(30.481)
$Hansard_{t-1}$	-0.023	(0.088)	0.379***	(0.075)	0.435***	(0.086)	0.298***	(0.075)
$Hansard_{t-2}$	0.122	(0.088)	0.067	(0.082)	0.109	(0.094)	-0.026	(0.080)
$Hansard_{t-3}$	-0.048	(0.088)	0.076	(0.076)	-0.042	(0.087)	-0.023	(0.074)
Committees	23.244[a]	(13.007)	-13.110	(9.571)	-15.254	(21.248)	-27.034	(23.679)
PMBills	-13.007	(22.263)	10.492**	(3.268)	–	–	85.072**	(29.828)
GVBills	–	–	11.995**	(3.546)	-2.963	(6.413)	-8.323	(10.520)
THSpeech	37.006	(68.248)	-17.369	(13.093)	15.558**	(5.571)	-10.359	(11.517)
Sit	0.872***	(0.257)	2.988**	(0.997)	1.528*	(0.584)	13.015***	(2.064)
R^2	0.125		0.478		0.322		0.437	

Independent variables	Inflation β	SE(β)	National unity β	SE(β)	Taxes β	SE(β)	Unemployment β	SE(β)
Constant	-0.585	(1.774)	-61.066	(49.090)	-65.547*	(32.766)	-71.173[a]	(42.512)
$Hansard_{t-1}$	0.260**	(0.079)	0.350***	(0.091)	0.295***	(0.080)	-0.022	(0.079)
$Hansard_{t-2}$	-0.029	(0.083)	0.168	(0.113)	0.027	(0.083)	0.163*	(0.077)
$Hansard_{t-3}$	-0.005	(0.078)	-0.066	(0.110)	0.175*	(0.078)	0.193*	(0.077)
Committees	–	–	115.503	(76.466)	-27.644	(26.446)	-47.874	(96.309)
PMBills	–	–	-13.320	(66.885)	-14.184	(25.785)	59.384	(44.776)
GVBills	–	–	-2.386	(24.597)	3.490	(8.049)	-16.697	(26.637)
THSpeech	49.975***	(8.643)	-8.435	(12.407)	62.439	(44.077)	50.554**	(18.730)
Sit	0.311*	(0.119)	12.142**	(3.551)	13.125***	(2.539)	16.010***	(2.886)
R^2	0.342		0.278		0.405		0.318	

Note: Cells contain coefficients from OLS regression coefficients with standard errors in parentheses, using monthly data from 1985 to 1995.

[a] $p < .10$, * $p < .05$, ** $p < .01$, *** $p < .001$

that Question Period content is modelled here as a function of past Question Period content and a variety of other policymaking indicators.

Creating the *Hansard* measure itself requires a certain amount of creativity. The House does not sit every day or every month, yet the series is used here and in later chapters as a monthly indication of the Question Period agenda. There are two ways in which the number of days sat per month can be built into the model. First, estimations can include a variable for the number of days the House sat each month. This variable *(Sit)* should soak up the effects of variations in monthly House business as well as the effects of months in which the House did not sit at all. Second, the number of column centimetres each month can be divided by the number of days. The first method is the simplest, and allows us to examine the coefficients and the effectiveness of the monthly adjustments. This is therefore the method used in the estimations below.

Current values of each of the independent variables are used, with the expectation that any effects should happen simultaneously, at least using monthly data. Since the model does not seek to estimate causality but only relationships between the series, this is not a problem. Three lags of the *Hansard* measure are also included, enough to soak up any autocorrelation in the series. The policy series, in fact, are very weakly autocorrelated, as the magnitude and significance of the lagged dependent variables in the estimations attest. None of the time series is nonstationary, and residuals tested negative in all cases for autocorrelation and heteroskedasticity. Again, all of these time series issues are described more thoroughly in Appendix A.

The results presented in Table 5.5 show that Question Period content reflects other measures of the policy agenda only intermittently. AIDS shows a weak effect of committee reports on Question Period, but this is the only issue that does. Private member's and government bills appear to affect Question Period discussion of crime, and only the former do so for environment. Throne Speech content is related to Question Period discussion of debt/deficit, inflation, and unemployment.

Admittedly, these are relatively weak tests for relationships between these other variables and the Question Period series; they allow only for simultaneous monthly effects, whereas the impact of these measures might take place over a longer period. Cross-correlation functions (CCFs), however (not presented here), did not indicate any longer-term correlations in either direction. In short, there are no clear trends, and while the analysis demonstrates that committee reports, bills, and Throne Speeches sometimes affect Question Period discussion, they also show that the Question Period analysis does not accurately reflect policymakers' activities in other venues.

Conceptual Considerations

This chapter has discussed and analyzed potential measures of the policy agenda in Canada. Thus far, however, it has concentrated on empirical investigation and ignored conceptual discussion about how and when measures are appropriate.

Work by Cobb and Elder is a good starting point. These authors distinguish between systemic and institutional policy agendas. The former refers to "a general set of political controversies that will be viewed at any point in time as falling within the range of legitimate concerns meriting the attention of the policy." The institutional agenda, on the other hand, is "a set of concrete, specific items scheduled for active and serious consideration by a particular institutional decision-making body" (Cobb and Elder 1972, 14). Pritchard and Berkowitz (1993, 86) suggest a similar distinction between symbolic and resource policy agendas: "Symbolic agendas are those lists of issues that require visible, but not necessarily substantive, action on the part of policy makers. Resource agendas are those lists of issues that require substantive action, including the possible allocation of resources." Symbolic agendas, they suggest, are much more flexible: it is easier to make a speech than to re-allocate resources.

While the two typologies differ slightly, they are similar in theme. Both pairs of authors agree that it is important to distinguish between different kinds of policy agendas, and each draws a line between an abstract attention-based agenda and a more concrete resource-oriented agenda. Moreover, both typologies point to the fact that attention is much more flexible, and likely more responsive to other agendas, than are resources.

How, then, are the various measures outlined above related to resource- and attention-based conceptions of the policy agenda, and what are the implications for empirical modelling? Question Period is clearly attention-based. It is therefore the most likely to react to other agendas, at least in the short term. Committee reports, legislation, and spending, on the other hand, are progressively more resource-oriented. These agendas will likely be less reactive to public and media agendas in the short term, although they may show a response over an extended period. Long-term public or media effects on committee activities or legislation are certainly possible, and a number of agenda studies have examined exactly this kind of impact (e.g., Page and Shapiro 1983). Any reaction of these measures may be too delayed to detect in an analysis spanning a short period, but committees and legislation can still have short-term effects on other agendas. The Question Period regressions show that these phenomena can intermittently affect Question Period discussion, but there is also the possibility that committee reports and legislative initiatives can affect the media, and subsequently the public, agenda. Their diminished role as dependent variables does not negate their importance as independent variables.

Analyses in later chapters use policy measures in the following ways. The Question Period measure is used as both a dependent and an independent variable; it is our primary measure of the policy agenda. When we are looking for the effects of the media or the public on government, Question Period is the most likely arena where these effects will first become evident. Question Period content is also an important independent variable. Past work indicates that it is the main forum through which policy discussion gets transmitted to the media.

Question Period content is not the only independent variable. Committee reports and discussion of government and private member's bills are also included as independent variables, with the expectation that, although their slow reaction time precludes using them as dependent variables in this study, they may still affect the media, public, and other policy agendas. Throne Speech content is also included as an independent variable. Its intermittent nature makes it difficult to use as a dependent variable, in spite of the fact that it more closely allied with symbolic than resource agendas. Nevertheless, the Question Period regressions indicate its potential role as an independent variable, and it is easily accommodated as such in the models that follow.

Summary and Conclusions

This investigation has illustrated the varied potential for five different measures of the Canadian policy agenda: government spending, committee activities, legislative initiatives, Throne Speech content, and Question Period discussion. The incremental changes that are typical of government spending make this measure unlikely to show any kind of short-term effects. Committees, legislation, and Throne Speeches are unlikely to be impacted by the media or public agendas in the short term but are potentially important independent variables. Question Period content, on the other hand, is an attention-based policy measure likely to both affect and be affected by other agendas.

An analysis of the relationship between Question Period and other policy indicators, however, demonstrates that a policy agenda measure based only on Question Period content misses part of the picture. If any conclusions can be drawn from this work, it is that different policy venues can exhibit different agendas, and that issue salience in different venues is loosely related at best. It is therefore important to incorporate a variety of policy measures into agenda-setting models, and the variation between them suggests that these measures should be included individually. The modelling in Chapters 6 and 7 will do exactly this.

6
Modelling Agenda-Setting

Who actually said, heard, felt, counted, named the thing about which you have an opinion? Was it the man who told you, or the man who told him, or someone still further removed? And how much was he permitted to see? When he informs you that France thinks this and that, what part of France did he watch? How was he able to watch it? Where was he when he watched it? What Frenchmen was he permitted to talk to, what newspapers did he read, and where did they learn what they say? You can ask yourself these questions, but can rarely answer them. They will remind you, however, of the distance which often separates your public opinion from the event with which it deals.

– Walter Lippmann (1922, 29)

Lippmann's warning may be well founded, but evidence below suggests that it should not be universally applied. Not only do the following results go some way towards answering Lippmann's first question – "Who actually said, heard, felt, counted, named the thing about which you have an opinion?" – but they also indicate that the distance between public opinion and reality is not always so great. Some issues are quite clearly real-world driven. On the other hand, the evidence here also points to systematic inter-issue differences in agenda-setting dynamics: some issues are real-world driven, some are first identified by policymakers, and others – as Lippmann suspected – provide strong confirmation of media influence.

Whereas previous chapters examine individual agendas in Canada, this chapter focuses on multi-agenda analyses. Results in previous chapters are now used as the methodological backbone for a grander objective: modelling the expanded agenda-setting process. The information accumulated thus far is used here to estimate interactions between the media, public, and policy agendas.

We begin with a description of the basic agenda-setting model, followed by brief reviews of the various agenda measures detailed in Chapters 3 to 5. As the centrepiece of this project, the estimations then take up the bulk of this chapter. Detailed results are presented for each of the eight issues, with an eye on the predominant causal effects. The end product is a body of results that (1) accurately describe agenda-setting dynamics for eight individual issues in Canada; (2) serve as tests of the prominent, sensational, and governmental issue types; and, more generally, (3) provide experiments into the value of an expanded agenda-setting estimation. The results indicate that both the issue types and expanded model are on solid ground. With only a few exceptions, issue dynamics tend to be of the sort described in Chapter 2, and these dynamics appear to be captured well in the seemingly unrelated regressions (SUR) estimations used below.

The Model

All the models in this chapter are estimated using Zellner-Aitken seemingly unrelated regressions (SUR). A detailed description of SUR methods is given in Appendix A as part of a more general account of time series methods in agenda-setting research. If the reader would like a more thorough review of statistical methods, Appendix A is a place to start. For the purposes of the current chapter, however, a basic understanding of SUR is assumed, and so we move directly to the three-equation agenda-setting model upon which subsequent work is premised:

$$MD_t = \alpha_1 + \sum_{k=1}^{K} \beta_{1(k)} MD_{t-k} + \sum_{k=1}^{K} \beta_{2(k)} PB_{t-k} + \sum_{k=1}^{K} \beta_{3(k)} QP_{t-k} \tag{6.1}$$
$$+ (\beta_4 Cm_{t-1} + \beta_5 Cm_t) + (\beta_6 Gb_{t-1} + \beta_7 Gb_t) + (\beta_8 PMb_{t-1} + \beta_9 PMb_t)$$
$$+ (\beta_{10} THSp_{t-1} + \beta_{11} THSp_t) + (\beta_{12} Ec_{t-1} + \beta_{13} Ec_t + \beta_{14} Ec_{t+1})$$
$$+ (\beta_{15} Bd_{t-1} + \beta_{16} Bd_t + \beta_{17} Bd_{t+1})$$
$$+ \sum_{m=1}^{M} \beta_{18(m)} RW_{t-m} + \varepsilon_{1t}$$

$$PB_t = \alpha_2 + \sum_{k=1}^{K} \beta_{19(k)} MD_{t-k} + \sum_{k=1}^{K} \beta_{20(k)} PB_{t-k} \tag{6.2}$$
$$+ (\beta_{21} Ec_{t-1} + \beta_{22} Ec_t + \beta_{23} Ec_{t+1})$$
$$+ \sum_{m=1}^{M} \beta_{24(m)} RW_{t-m} + \varepsilon_{2t}$$

$$QP_t = \alpha_3 + \sum_{k=1}^{K} \beta_{25(k)} MD_{t-k} + \sum_{k=1}^{K} \beta_{26(k)} PB_{t-k} + \sum_{k=1}^{K} \beta_{27(k)} QP_{t-k} \qquad (6.3)$$

$$+ (\beta_{28} Cm_{t-1} + \beta_{29} Cm_t) + (\beta_{30} Gb_{t-1} + \beta_{31} Gb_t) + (\beta_{32} PMb_{t-1} + \beta_{33} PMb_t)$$

$$+ (\beta_{34} THSp_{t-1} + \beta_{35} THSp_t) + (\beta_{36} Bd_{t-1} + \beta_{37} Bd_t + \beta_{38} Bd_{t+1}) + \beta_{39} Sit_t$$

$$+ \sum_{m=1}^{M} \beta_{40(m)} RW_{t-m} + \varepsilon_{3t}$$

MD (media), PB (public), and QP (policy) are the endogenous variables described in previous chapters. MD is the number of issue-related stories, monthly, in eight major Canadian newspapers. PB is the proportion of responses to the "most important problem" (MIP) question citing the relevant issue. QP is the number of column centimetres in *Hansard* dealing with the issue during Question Period.

This system of equations represents an effort to capture the dynamics illustrated in Figure 1.1 (page 11). Simply put, the model attempts to predict current values for each of the endogenous variables (media content, public opinion, and Question Period content) using past values of these endogenous, and a number of additional exogenous, variables. Both of the other agendas are included in the media and policy equations. Only the media are included in the public agenda equation, since the vast majority of individuals will not directly experience the policy agenda. Policy agenda effects on the public, then, can occur only via the media agenda.

The number of lags (k) used for these three endogenous variables is different for each issue, and was determined using what has become the usual strategy to establish lag length in vector autoregression (VAR)/SUR estimations. First, the model is estimated using a maximum number of lags, where the maximum is based on either data constraints or theoretical premise. In this case, the initial number of lags was six, with the assumption that any impact of one agenda on another would happen within a six-month period. Next, the statistical significance of the sixth lag of all endogenous variables is tested using a Granger exogeneity test. If the lag is not statistically significant, it is dropped. Subsequent lags are dropped using the same process, until a statistically significant lag is reached (see Enders 1996). This model's residuals are then tested for autocorrelation; if no autocorrelation exists, the model is accepted. Using this method, the environment and inflation models use five lags, and the others use three.

The model also incorporates a variety of exogenous variables, including the additional policy-related measures described in Chapter 5. A committee reports variable (*Cm*) counts the number of related reports presented in the House each month; private member's and government bills variables (*PMb* and *Gb*) count the number of bill discussions (first, second, third, and other readings) in the House each month; the Throne Speech variable (*THSp*) is the proportion of the speech given to an issue in months when there was a Throne Speech, and is coded as zero in all other months. Preliminary tests showed that any correlation between these policy variables and the others exists either concurrently or within a one-month period. Accordingly, they are included at lags t and $t-1$ only. It is assumed that, like *Hansard*, these policy variables cannot affect public opinion directly. Accordingly, they are included only in the media and policy equations. Finally, these exogenous policy series are included only for issues where relevant series exist. There are no reports or bills that are relevant to inflation, for instance, so these variables are excluded from the inflation estimations.

The estimations also include dummy variables for elections (*Ec*) and budgets (*Bd*). These can be seen as "structural" policy variables, which do not reflect any measure of government attention. These variables may nevertheless have an effect on attention to issues, and so are included here both to test this possibility and to control for these effects in the larger estimation. Since the House does not usually sit for several months before or after an election, the election variable is included in the media and public equations only. Budgets, on the other hand, should not affect the public directly, so this variable is included in the media and policy equations only. Preliminary tests showed that any election and budget effects also happen within a one-month period, but that the impact of these phenomena sometimes precedes the actual event. The effect of elections on the public, for instance, can occur during the campaign period in the month preceding the actual vote. Similarly, anticipation of the April budget can often have an effect on Question Period discussion in March. Election and budget variables, then, are included at lags $t-1$, t, and $t+1$. A dummy variable for months in which the House did not sit at all *(Sit)* is also included in equation 6.3, to soak up the effects of months in which there was no potential for a *Hansard* measure score anything other than zero.

Finally, most models include real-world indicators *(RW)*. The only exception is national unity, for which there is no available real-world indicator. Ideally, it would be possible to use opinion on separation in Quebec as an exogenous measure in this estimation, thereby examining whether media, government, and national public concern over national unity is related to Quebeckers' support for independence. Cloutier et al.'s history (1992) of sovereignty support in Quebec shows, unfortunately, that polls during this period are too sparse to build an adequate longitudinal measure.

The other seven models, on the other hand, include at least one real-world measure:

AIDS: Yearly change in number of AIDS cases.
Crime: Yearly change in violent crime rate; yearly change in property crime rate.

Debt/deficit: Yearly change in debt as a proportion of GDP; yearly change in deficit as a proportion of federal government spending.

Environment: Yearly change in number of hectares harvested (forests); yearly change in ozone-depleting substances; yearly change in carbon dioxide emissions; yearly change in number of species at risk.

Inflation: Monthly change in consumer price index (CPI).

Taxes: Yearly change in income tax burden; yearly change in consumption tax burden.

Unemployment: Monthly change in unemployment rate.

Detailed information on the calculation and sources of real-world indicators is provided in Appendix E. Differenced series (yearly or monthly *changes,* rather than levels) are used based on the belief that reactions by the public, media, and policymakers will most often be to relative changes in the various real-world indicators rather than to their actual values. The number of lags for real-world variables (m) varies across issues, but is based on the same process as for the endogenous variables (k) – analyses began with six lags and subtracted lags if they were not statistically significant based on Granger exogeneity tests.

The overall models, then, test two different groups of hypotheses. First, they test the inter-relationships between media content, public opinion, and Question Period discussion. These tests are pertinent to the issue types described in Chapter 2, and represent the culmination of work on an "expanded," multidirectional agenda-setting process. Second, these models test the degree to which a wide variety of other variables are related to this process. Committees, bills, Throne Speeches, elections, budgets, and real-world factors may have varying effects on the three endogenous variables. Including them in equations 6.1 to 6.3 both estimates the significance of these effects and controls for these variables in measuring media-public–Question Period dynamics.

The estimations themselves are not presented here, since coefficients are not necessarily readily interpretable.[1] This is due in part to potential multicollinearity; because most models include a relatively small number of lags, however, multicollinearity problems are minimized. A more fundamental problem in interpreting the coefficients, discussed in Appendix A, is that the equations are solved as a system. Accordingly, effects of one variable on another can occur both directly and indirectly. For instance, the model accounts for the possibility that the public can affect policymakers

---

[1]   Some results from the estimations are reported in Soroka 1999a; all are available from the author upon request.

directly or can affect them indirectly by affecting the media, which subsequently affect policymakers. The raw coefficients provide little information about the indirect effects, then. Where a relatively small number of lags is used, the magnitude or direction of a single coefficient can be a useful indicator. For the most part, however, the estimations themselves provide little information that is not more easily – and accurately – interpreted using other methods.

The methods used below are (1) graphs of the time series themselves, (2) Granger exogeneity tests, and (3) impulse response functions. The latter two exhibits are drawn from the results of the model described in equations 6.1 to 6.3, and the methods are described in detail in Appendix A. It is worth noting that while the two should certainly be related, Granger tests and impulse response functions will not always show exactly the same dynamics. As with the coefficients themselves, Granger exogeneity tests speak only to direct effects, whereas impulse response functions are a more appropriate method for considering both direct *and* indirect effects. Accordingly, the analyses will consider both, taking advantage of the easy interpretation offered by the Granger tests, and the consideration of both direct and indirect effects afforded by the impulse response functions.

Results

The hypotheses about issue types described in Chapter 2 are largely supported by the results that follow. There are two exceptions: both AIDS and crime show comparatively little variation in public opinion over the time period, making an accurate estimation of effects difficult. The other six issues, however, are relatively free of data problems and provide illustrations both of the three issue types and of the potential of the expanded model and SUR estimation used here.

Prominent Issues

Both inflation and unemployment offer strong illustrations of prominent-issue dynamics. Figure 6.1 displays the time series for inflation. Inflation can be divided into two periods from 1985 to 1995: a pre-1991 period of rising inflation and increased public concern about inflation, and a post-1991 period of lower inflation and lower public concern. The media series in Figure 6.1 appears to follow a connected but slightly different path.

The situation for unemployment is very similar (see Figure 6.2). As with inflation, there is a strong relationship between the public agenda and the unemployment rate. In this case, both series start high, reach a low point around 1990, and then steadily increase until 1995. Policy and media attention to unemployment follow similar but less pronounced trends. The exception to the rule is a spike in the media agenda in 1989, the product of unemployment policy discussions that were especially salient in *La Presse*.

Figure 6.1

Inflation: time series

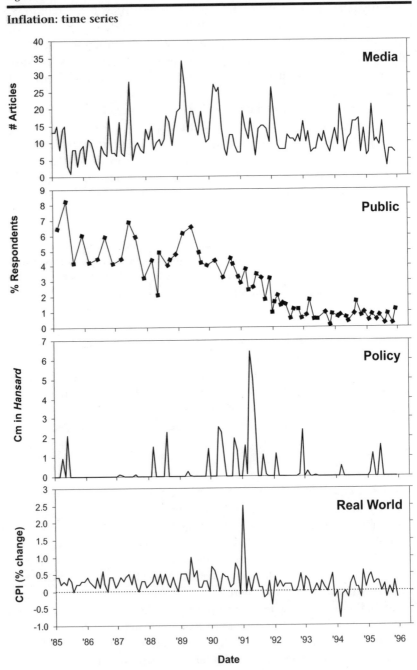

Figure 6.2

Unemployment: time series

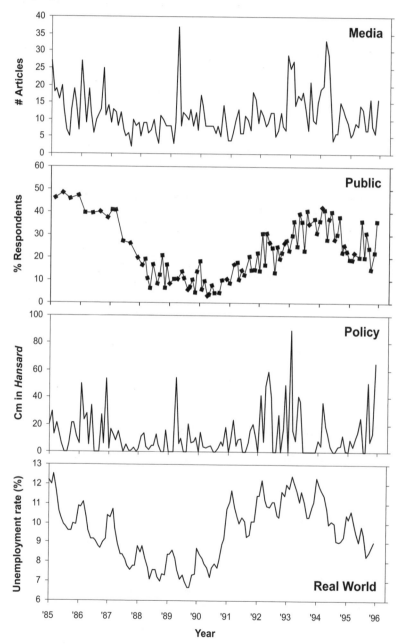

The dynamics suggested by the inflation and unemployment time series are borne out in the Granger exogeneity tests displayed in Table 6.1. Each dependent variable is listed along with all its independents. The chi-square (χ^2) test tests the null hypothesis that the coefficients for all lags of that independent variable are not different from zero. A significant chi-square test indicates that lags of the independent variable contribute statistically significant information to the prediction of the dependent variable, above and beyond the effects of all the other variables in the system.

The Granger tests show that the endogenous series are autocorrelated. Each series' past values are significant predictors of its current value – the media coefficients are significant in the media equations, the public coefficients

Table 6.1

Directions of causality: prominent issues

		Issue			
Variable		Inflation		Unemployment	
Dependent	Independent	χ^2	p	χ^2	p
Media	Media	**40.773**	**(0.000)**	**14.559**	**(0.002)**
	Public	6.688	(0.245)	**10.036**	**(0.018)**
	Policy	9.921	(0.078)	1.384	(0.709)
	Committees	–	–	1.464	(0.481)
	Bills	–	–	**18.251**	**(0.001)**
	Throne Speech	0.191	(0.909)	**25.485**	**(0.000)**
	Election	3.151	(0.369)	3.158	(0.368)
	Budget	**30.937**	**(0.000)**	2.700	(0.440)
	Real world	5.849	(0.211)	**8.522**	**(0.074)**
Public	Media	2.285	(0.809)	2.146	(0.543)
	Public	**1086.025**	**(0.000)**	**584.911**	**(0.000)**
	Election	1.358	(0.715)	5.444	(0.142)
	Real world	**12.811**	**(0.012)**	**10.702**	**(0.030)**
Policy	Media	5.541	(0.353)	4.451	(0.217)
	Public	**15.062**	**(0.010)**	3.971	(0.265)
	Policy	**10.522**	**(0.062)**	6.010	(0.111)
	Committees	–	–	**5.355**	**(0.069)**
	Bills	–	–	1.391	(0.846)
	Throne Speech	**29.109**	**(0.000)**	**14.154**	**(0.001)**
	Budget	5.992	(0.112)	3.023	(0.388)
	Real world	**65.067**	**(0.000)**	**18.810**	**(0.001)**
Period		85:5 to 95:11		85:6 to 95:11	
Lags/df		5		3	

Note: Cells contain chi-square (χ^2) results, with p values in parentheses, from Granger causality tests based on a SUR estimation of equations 6.1 to 6.3, using monthly data from 1985 to 1995. Text in bold is significant at $p < .10$.

in the public equations, and the policy coefficients in the policy equations. The only exception is the policy agenda for unemployment, which narrowly misses statistical significance ($p = .111$).

More interesting, however, is the fact that real-world indicators are significant predictors of issue salience for both issues. Granger tests of real-world lags indicate that the salience of inflation on public and policy agendas is led by changes in the CPI, and that the salience of unemployment on all three agendas is led by the unemployment rate. It is worth noting that real-world effects for unemployment are stronger for the public and policy agendas than for the media agenda (the latter is significant only at $p = .074$); nevertheless, effects exist in all three cases.

Some other effects are also evident. Budgets spark attention to inflation in the media, for instance, while Throne Speech content creates a similar rise in attention during Question Period. For unemployment, committee reports, bills, and Throne Speech content spark interest in either the media or policy agenda. These effects signal the value of including additional policy measures in the estimations. Each can affect media and Question Period content, and further analysis may reveal that these effects are systematic or predictable.

Finally, there is a significant effect of the public on the policy agenda for inflation and on the media agenda for unemployment. This is likely an indication that the public reacts early to real-world indicators, and that policy and/or media responses are both to real-world factors and to the public's reaction to them.

This trend is clearer in the impulse response functions, shown in Figure 6.3. Three graphs are displayed for each issue. The first illustrates the effects on each agenda of a one standard deviation impulse in the media agenda, and the other two do the same for the public and policy agendas. (The decomposition used to estimate impulse response functions is described in Appendix A.)

As in the Granger exogeneity tests, the public graphs for both issues indicate a relatively high degree of autocorrelation in the public agenda series. Each also shows temporary impacts of the public agenda on the media agenda, and the unemployment graph shows a small impact on the policy agenda at periods 2 and 3. Again, these effects are likely the product of the public being the first to react to rising inflation and unemployment, and media/policymakers subsequently reacting to both real-world indicators and public concern.

There are few additional effects. There is a slight, inconsistent impact of policy on the media agenda for inflation, and media series for both issues have small effects on the other two agendas. For the most part, however, few inter-agenda effects exist; the salience of prominent issues is driven primarily by real-world indicators.

Figure 6.3

Prominent issues: impulse response functions

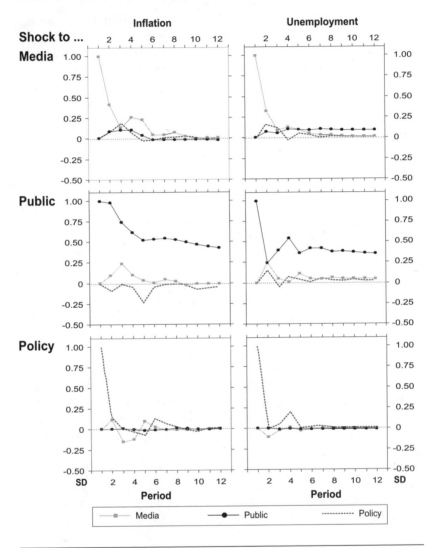

Thus, the evidence presented here corroborates earlier research that found few agenda-setting effects for inflation and unemployment. In short, issues that are experienced every day are much less open to media influence. This is not to say that such prominent issues are never open to media influence, but this topic will be left for Chapter 7. In the meantime, it is clear that inflation and unemployment are accurately portrayed as prominent issues – issues that tend to display few agenda-setting effects above and beyond each series' autocorrelation and the significant effects of real-world indicators.

Sensational Issues

Data were gathered for three sensational issues: AIDS, crime, and environment. Unfortunately, the variation in public opinion for both AIDS and crime from 1985 to 1995 is very low. In spite of considerable media attention, AIDS is never cited by more than 2% of respondents to the MIP question, and crime never exceeds 8%. This makes measuring the impact on or of public opinion difficult: what little variation can exist is more likely random error than an indication of changing salience.

In the case of AIDS, it may be that attention to some issues simply cannot be adequately measured with the MIP question. Proving this hypothesis would require further analysis; if it is true, some agenda-setting analyses will have to rely on more subject-specific questions to more accurately measure changing salience for the public. Unfortunately, there is no such question for AIDS during this time period. It should have been telling, perhaps, that Rogers et al.'s detailed study (1991) of agenda-setting in the US for AIDS makes only a minimal effort to deal with the public agenda. The salience of crime, on the other hand, does show up in MIP responses, just not in Canada during this time period. Crime may simply not have been salient enough to provide adequate variance in public opinion in this country.

An alternative hypothesis is that the AIDS and crime estimations are plagued by gradually rising trends in salience. While other issues rise and fall during the survey period, the salience of crime rises gradually and consistently and the salience of AIDS is consistently declining (since there was no public opinion measure before 1989). Statistically speaking, highly autocorrelated (integrated) series may be creating estimation problems. Econometricians are divided, however, on the question of using integrated series in VAR/SUR models (see Doan 1996, ch. 8).

Although not presented here, estimations were performed for both AIDS and crime. No inter-agenda effects were identified for AIDS except for an impact of the public on the media agenda. The crime estimation showed evidence of various effects: there was some evidence of a media impact on policy, as expected for a sensational issue, and again evidence of a public impact on media content. This is clearly not the direction of influence predicted for sensational issues, so either AIDS and crime are not sensational issues or there are other problems with the estimations. In any case, one cannot have too much confidence in estimations that rely on a public opinion measure with a constant trend and extremely high autocorrelation.

In sum, results for AIDS and crime (or the lack thereof) could be (1) a product of data problems created by little variance or a steady trend, or (2) an accurate reflection of the role the public can play in issues whose salience experiences gradual change. Determining which explanation is correct will be left to further research. Data problems might be considered, such as the effects of integrated series on VAR/SUR estimations. Otherwise, we might consider why public opinion shows little change for these issues despite considerable swings in media attention. We should not dismiss the possibility that the media simply did not have an effect on the public agenda for AIDS and crime, and that the public agenda was driven by and large by itself – issues developed in the public independent of media and policy agenda attention. The chapter will refrain from drawing such inferences, however. Further testing is required to draw accurate conclusions about the agenda-setting dynamics surrounding the AIDS and crime issues. (We will return to modelling agenda-setting dynamics for AIDS in Chapter 7.)

As a result, environment is left as the sole example of a sensational issue in the current analysis. Past agenda-setting work on the environment has shown this issue to consistently exhibit public agenda-setting effects by the media. Moreover, Figure 6.4 displays what appears to be a classic public agenda-setting time series. Environment begins low on the public and media agendas, rising quickly in the late 1980s, and then gradually declining to what appears to be an equilibrium slightly higher than before.

Indeed, the Granger tests in Table 6.2 also present evidence of the typical public agenda-setting model. The media agenda has a significant impact on both the public and policy agendas. This is also reflected in the impulse response functions in Figure 6.5: a rise in media attention leads to increases in both public and policy attention. The impact on the public agenda is relatively small but long-lived, declining gradually until period 12.

That said, media effects are only part of the story. The public agenda affects the policy agenda at period 2, and has a delayed but significant impact on the media agenda as well. The policy agenda also has a weak influence on media attention at period 2. These effects are also evident in the Granger tests: all the endogenous series are significant predictors in all three equations. Thus, the media play a significant role in increased attention to environmental issues, but results indicate that the media, the public, and policymakers likely play mutually reinforcing roles.

While unidirectional effects of the media on other agendas are not identified in this model, additional considerations do suggest the comparative significance of the media as a leader over the public and policy agendas. Impulse response functions suggest that media effects on the public, for instance, begin at period 2 and are lasting. Public effects on the media, on the other hand, are initially negative and do not become positive until period 4. These dynamics suggest the possibility that while the relationship between the media and the public becomes a reciprocal one, the initial relationship is one in which the media lead.

Figure 6.4

Environment: time series

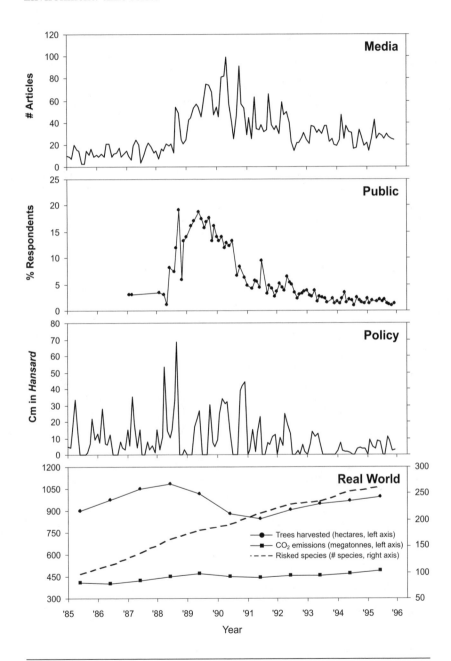

Table 6.2

Directions of causality: sensational issues

Variable		Issue	
		Environment	
Dependent	Independent	χ^2	p
Media	Media	**10.855**	**(0.054)**
	Public	**14.339**	**(0.014)**
	Policy	**18.788**	**(0.002)**
	Committees	1.981	(0.371)
	Bills	**14.198**	**(0.007)**
	Throne Speech	**13.721**	**(0.001)**
	Election	0.232	(0.972)
	Budget	**17.607**	**(0.001)**
	Real world	6.931	(0.140)
Public	Media	**10.804**	**(0.055)**
	Public	**65.765**	**(0.000)**
	Election	**13.126**	**(0.004)**
	Real world	**33.928**	**(0.000)**
Policy	Media	**14.780**	**(0.011)**
	Public	**18.513**	**(0.002)**
	Policy	**16.833**	**(0.005)**
	Committees	1.877	(0.391)
	Bills	6.952	(0.138)
	Throne Speech	1.457	(0.483)
	Budget	3.383	(0.336)
	Real world	**13.822**	**(0.008)**
Period		87:8 to 95:11	
Lags/df		5	

Note: Cells contain chi-square (χ^2) results, with p values in parentheses, from Granger causality tests based on a SUR estimation of equations 6.1 to 6.3, using monthly data from 1985 to 1995. Text in bold is significant at $p < .10$.

Figure 6.5

Sensational issues: impulse response functions

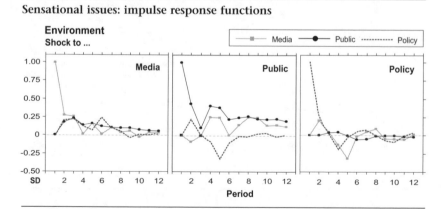

In terms of the media-policy link, impulse response functions indicate that media effects on policymakers are slightly greater and more prolonged than are effects in the other direction. The predominant direction of the media-policy relationship, however, can be determined in a more convincing manner using weekly series. While the larger estimations use monthly data, after all, both the media and policy time series are available on a weekly basis, which may provide a more accurate look at inter-agenda dynamics. Granger causality tests with these weekly data using four lags indicate that media Granger-causes policy and that policy does not Granger-cause media ($F = 2.274$; $p = .06$; df = 4,558). As with the public, then, and demonstrated in a more compelling fashion, the media plays the dominant role in the media-policy relationship, in line with our expectations for sensational issues.

Governmental Issues

The time series for three governmental issues – debt/deficit, taxes, and national unity – are displayed in Figures 6.6, 6.7, and 6.8. Each shows considerable variation in issue salience in all three agendas. For debt/deficit, the sharp increase in the policy series in 1989 marks the Throne Speech that introduced debt/deficit to the media, public, and policy agendas (Figure 6.6). The salience of debt/deficit issues then declines gradually until the 1993 election, when there is a marked rise in issue salience for all three agenda series.

The taxes time series in Figure 6.7 look remarkably similar to the environment series. Taxes are low on the media and public agendas, rising abruptly in the late 1980s and then slowly declining to a level in the mid-1990s that, for the media at least, is slightly higher than the level before the increased salience. All three series show a prolonged period of high salience from 1989 to 1991, the period of debate surrounding the new GST.

The national unity time series indicate three periods of increased salience. The first is in 1987, when the Meech Lake Accord led to increases in both the media and policy agendas. The second and more prolonged period begins in 1990, when the Meech Lake Accord failed and we entered the period leading up to the Charlottetown Accord referendum. Finally, the rise in 1995 reflects the Quebec referendum that year. The way in which the public series appears to follow the media series is remarkable, and foreshadows the importance of media content in the national unity estimation.

Granger results for these three issues are shown in Table 6.3. In all cases, the tests demonstrate the importance of the media agenda. Media lags are significant predictors in all three equations for national unity and taxes; in spite of there being little autocorrelation in the media agenda for debt/deficit, media lags are nevertheless significant in the public and policy equations. Impulse response functions also illustrate the importance of

Figure 6.6

Debt/deficit: time series

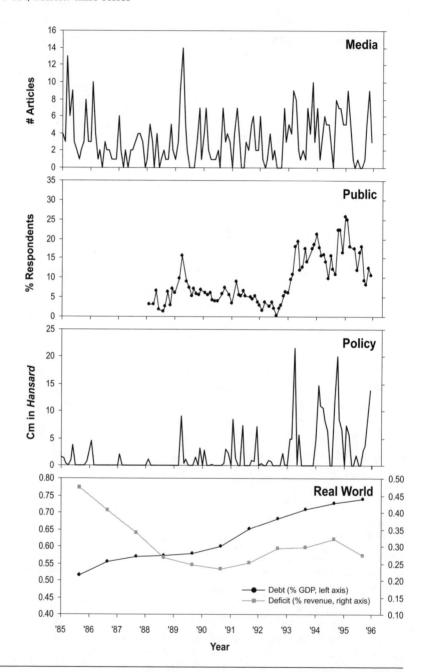

Figure 6.7

Taxes: time series

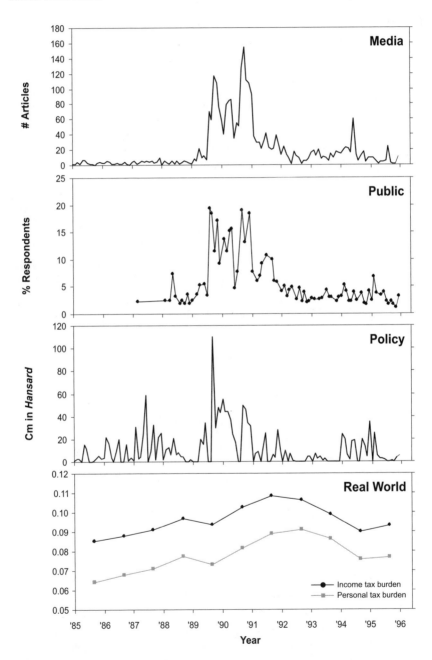

Figure 6.8

National unity: time series

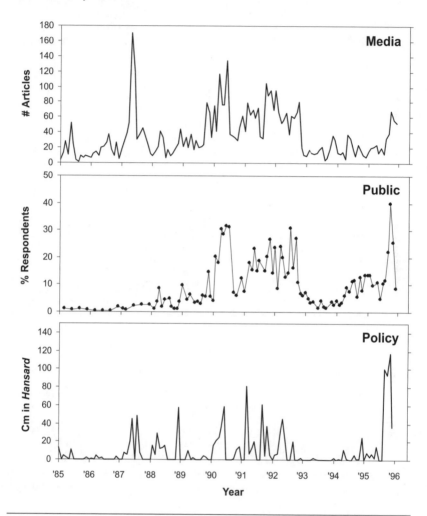

the media agenda (Figure 6.9). An increase in the salience of debt/deficit or national unity issues for the media leads to marked and sustained increases in salience for the public agenda, and all three issues show (admittedly variable) impacts of media content on policy agendas.

The expected policy effects on media content are less clear. For taxes, Granger tests show that Question Period content is a significant predictor of media content, and that the media agenda subsequently affects public opinion. These effects are only mildly reflected in the impulse response functions, but the temporary effects of policy on media content at period 2 and the mild effects of media on public opinion at periods 2 and 3 reflect the trends indicated in the Granger results.

The case that taxes are a policy-driven issue is buttressed by the very strong effect an impact on the public series has on both the media and policy agendas. Public reaction to the GST was considerable and sustained, and the content of the media and Question Period appears to have reacted

Figure 6.9

Governmental issues: impulse response functions

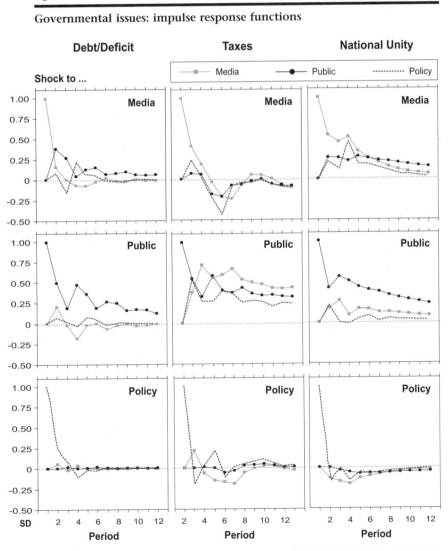

Table 6.3

Directions of causality: governmental issues

Variable		Issue					
		Debt/deficit		Taxes		National unity	
Dependent	Independent	χ^2	p	χ^2	p	χ^2	p
Media	Media	3.095	(0.377)	13.512	(0.019)	53.947	(0.000)
	Public	5.588	(0.133)	23.136	(0.000)	8.255	(0.041)
	Policy	0.570	(0.903)	18.676	(0.002)	4.931	(0.177)
	Committees	1.034	(0.596)	2.702	(0.259)	7.527	(0.023)
	Bills	1.526	(0.466)	2.362	(0.670)	7.855	(0.097)
	Throne Speech	8.016	(0.018)	3.254	(0.197)	0.583	(0.747)
	Election	5.557	(0.135)	0.268	(0.966)	0.926	(0.819)
	Budget	5.800	(0.122)	0.205	(0.977)	6.563	(0.087)
	Real world	2.899	(0.235)	11.997	(0.002)	–	–
	Economy	3.711	(0.294)	–	–	–	–
	Qref	–	–	–	–	3.243	(0.356)
	Nref	–	–	–	–	3.287	(0.349)
Public	Media	16.485	(0.001)	15.928	(0.007)	12.943	(0.005)
	Public	64.539	(0.000)	35.236	(0.000)	136.692	(0.000)
	Election	2.274	(0.517)	0.620	(0.892)	0.800	(0.849)
	Real world	0.224	(0.894)	2.214	(0.331)	–	–
	Economy	5.323	(0.150)	–	–	–	–
	Qref	–	–	–	–	38.923	(0.000)
	Nref	–	–	–	–	15.529	(0.001)

Policy	88:5 to 95:11		87:8 to 95:11		85:6 to 95:11	
Media	**10.911**	**(0.012)**	**18.125**	**(0.003)**	**25.263**	**(0.000)**
Public	0.690	(0.876)	**23.533**	**(0.000)**	6.328	(0.097)
Policy	**6.299**	**(0.098)**	**11.655**	**(0.040)**	4.802	(0.187)
Committees	0.550	(0.760)	0.664	(0.718)	0.854	(0.653)
Bills	**11.824**	**(0.003)**	6.538	(0.162)	**9.517**	**(0.049)**
Throne Speech	1.743	(0.418)	1.209	(0.546)	1.509	(0.470)
Budget	5.386	(0.146)	6.145	(0.105)	**6.472**	**(0.091)**
Real world	2.321	(0.313)	**21.637**	**(0.000)**	–	–
Economy	**10.081**	**(0.018)**	–	–	–	–
Qref	–	–	–	–	**129.900**	**(0.000)**
Nref	–	–	–	–	5.034	(0.169)
Period	88:5 to 95:11		87:8 to 95:11		85:6 to 95:11	
Lags/df	3		3		3	

Note: Cells contain chi-square (χ^2) results, with p values in parentheses, from Granger causality tests based on a SUR estimation of equations 6.1 to 6.3, using monthly data from 1985 to 1995. Text in bold is significant at $p < .10$. *Qref* is a dummy variable representing the 1995 Quebec referendum; *Nref* is a dummy variable representing the 1992 Charlottetown Accord referendum.

accordingly. If we consider the fact that the public was reacting to public policy, the impulse response functions stand as evidence that tax issues were policy-driven. The fact that effects of the policy agenda are not more adequately illustrated by policy variables, however, suggests that future analyses might consider how the policy agenda is specified. There is little doubt, for instance, that combining the GST bill with other tax-related bills reduced the chances of finding significant policy effects in this estimation. Nevertheless, both the Granger results and impulse response functions suggest that the salience of taxes for the public and media was driven at least in part by Question Period content.

Discovering evidence of a policy impact for debt/deficit and national unity is more difficult. In neither case is Question Period an adequate predictor of media content. For debt/deficit, a more conspicuous effect of policy on the media agenda takes the form of a strong and significant Throne Speech coefficient at lag 0 (β = 0.813, SE[β] = 0.305, $p < .05$) and, consequently, a significant Granger test for Throne Speech coefficients in Table 6.3. The significant effects here are likely entirely attributable to the 1989 Throne Speech. Interestingly, this Throne Speech variable is not a significant predictor for the Question Period series. Nevertheless, the Speech appears to have sparked media attention to the issue, and we can hypothesize that subsequent attention is in large part a product of this increased media attention.

The significant Throne Speech coefficient is evidence of two things. First, it is likely that debt/deficit is appropriately portrayed in Chapter 2 as a governmental issue. The media drove public attention to debt/deficit issues after 1989, but media attention was sparked by the 1989 Throne Speech. Second, and more generally speaking, these results emphasize the potential problems with using only one measure as an indication of the policy agenda. Granger tests, after all, show a unidirectional effect of media agenda on Question Period content. Without the additional policy measures, we would miss an important part of the picture of the dynamics surrounding debt/deficit issues in Canada.

Returning finally to national unity, significant Granger tests for bills and budgets constitute the only evidence of a policy effect on media content. Both Granger tests and impulse response functions show a much stronger media effect on policy. Impulse response functions, for instance, show a media impact leading to rise in the policy agenda that lasts until period 12, while a policy impact has virtually no effect on any agenda (and any effects on the media series are negative). As with environmental issues, weekly time series were used here in an effort to find Question Period effects on the media agenda, but the unidirectional effects indicated in the initial Granger tests remained.

In an effort to better model concern for national unity, this model also includes two additional dummy variables for the 1992 national referendum and the 1995 Quebec referendum. Granger tests show that both referenda coincided with increased public concern for national unity issues, and the Quebec referendum had a strong effect on attention to national unity in Question Period. Neither event seems to have affected media attention, however. This seems highly unlikely, but there are two possible explanations: (1) referendum-related articles included different keywords from those used for the national unity search, or (2) the increased salience for the media was for a longer period than is covered by the referendum dummy variables.

In sum, the models for governmental issues are similar in that they indicate both the potential lead role of the media and the difficulties with measuring and attributing cause to the policy agenda. It is possible to sort through the various measures and dynamics, and the models here indicate that effects are of the sort we would expect from governmental issues. In no case, however, is this conclusion an obvious one. Moreover, the differences between these governmental issues and the estimation for environment is not as clear as we would like. Despite weekly results showing that media led Question Period content, the environment estimation still shows significant effects for bills and budgets on media attention. (Throne Speeches also have a statistically significant Granger test, but coefficients are negative.) In short, the relative weakness of policy agenda effects makes it difficult to portray these issues as governmental. The debt/deficit story rests on a significant Granger test for Throne Speech content, while the taxes story relies on a weak but apparent connection between Question Period content, media content, and public opinion. The national unity estimation is the least successful; fortunately, results in Chapter 7 help to clarify the situation.

Summary and Conclusions

Tables 6.1 to 6.3 and Figures 6.1 to 6.9 present a considerable amount of information about issue dynamics in Canada from 1985 to 1995. They indicate, for instance, that inflation and unemployment display exactly what the prominent issue type leads us to expect. These issues are real-world driven, with little room for other dynamics. Environment, on the other hand, demonstrates considerable media impact, as anticipated in Chapter 2's description of sensational issues. Debt/deficit appears to be a good illustration of governmental issue dynamics: media content, sparked by the 1989 Throne Speech, led public attention.

While the model described in this chapter has its successes, however, it is not without difficulties. AIDS and crime estimations reveal few agenda-setting effects, despite the expectation that both issues would be media-driven. Whether this is a product of data or an accurate reflection of reality is unknown and will require further testing. National unity, on the other hand, displays the opposite effect to what was predicted: media appears to have led policy. In fact, each of the governmental issue estimations is testament to the difficulties involved in developing policy measures to use in agenda-setting analyses.

Generally speaking, the estimations in this chapter are successful in their attempt to both demonstrate the potential for this type of modelling and indicate the value of the prominent/sensational/governmental issue typology. The evidence here indicates that issue attributes have a clear and systematic effect on the agenda-setting process, and the SUR modelling demonstrates the value of identifying, rather than assuming, directions of causality. While these estimations are more comprehensive in both methodology and scope than most previous modelling efforts, however, still more can be done. This is the goal of Chapter 7.

7
Expanding the Models

Public perception of most "crises" in American domestic life does not reflect changes in real conditions as much as it reflects the operation of a systematic cycle of heightening public interest and then increasing boredom with major issues.

– Anthony Downs (1972, 39)

The analyses in Chapter 6 make a number of assumptions. They use all available data from 1985 to 1995, for instance, assuming that estimations will benefit from using the largest time period for which data are available. Multiple policy agendas are included in the model, but the media agenda measure is premised on the idea that media effects are best modelled using a single time series. And, in addressing agenda-setting in Canada, models in Chapter 6 assume that only Canadian agendas are pertinent.

This chapter challenges those assumptions. The goal here is not to prove that the models are wrong. Rather, it is suggested that, while the general model estimated in Chapter 6 is widely applicable and results provide accurate estimates of issue dynamics over an extended time period, improvements can be made on an issue-by-issue basis. The central goal of this chapter, then, is to further indicate the value of an expanded agenda-setting analysis: once a general model is established, the model can be tailored to offer particular insights into the agenda-setting dynamics of individual issues.

Accordingly, this chapter considers the individual traits of particular issues and suggests adjustments to the Chapter 6 models. First, we consider the possibility that issue dynamics will change over time. Prominent issues will vary in their prominence, for instance, and evidence here indicates that the potential for media influence varies as well. Second, this chapter tests the hypothesis that the age of issues affects inter-agenda dynamics. In the quotation at the beginning of this chapter, Downs (1972) suggests that increased issue salience has a limited lifespan. Evidence is presented here supporting both this proposition and Zucker's hypothesis (1978) that a newer issue is more open to agenda-setting effects.

Finally, the potential for additional exogenous variables is addressed. The media agenda is dissected again, this time with an eye on the *Globe and Mail* as a "leading" newspaper. Another, more interesting possibility is that the *New York Times* is a leading newspaper in Canada – there are several issues in which we might expect the Canadian media, public, and even policymakers to be affected by American media. A large proportion of television programming, both entertainment and news, originates in the US, and significant American newspapers such as the *New York Times* enjoy considerable Canadian circulation. Moreover, Canadian networks and newspapers may take cues from their more dominant American counterparts. The *New York Times*, then, may play a leading role, not only for Canadian media but also for the Canadian public. In view of this possibility, the final section of this chapter tests for evidence of cross-border agenda-setting.

Temporal Changes in Issue Prominence: Inflation and Unemployment

In an analysis of inflation in the 1960s and 1970s, MacKuen and Coombs (1981) find that dividing their time period into two intervals leads to dramatically different results. While the initial model appeared to be real-world driven, a model for the period of comparatively low inflation indicates media influence on the public agenda. These authors suggest that real-world factors lead when they are prominent, but that the media have the opportunity to lead when real-world indicators are less consequential.

The data used in preceding chapters offer an opportunity to replicate MacKuen and Coombs's analysis. The opportunity is attractive not only for the sake of replication but also because demonstrating media effects in periods of low real-world salience would be a further indication of the important role that prominence plays in agenda-setting dynamics.

The new inflation targets set in 1991 led to a lower rate of inflation from then onward, so problems with inflation were greater in the first half of the 1985-95 period than in the second. We might expect, then, that the potential for media influence was greater in the 1990s, when inflation itself was less prominent. Unemployment should show a similar change during periods of low salience: 1988-91 was a period of comparatively low unemployment, so the potential for media effects should have been greatest at this time.

In order to test this hypothesis, SUR models were re-estimated for inflation and unemployment. For inflation, cases were dropped on a month-by-month basis from the beginning of the series. For unemployment, cases were dropped from the beginning and end of the series. If there is in fact media influence in periods of low prominence, this should be reflected in the results.

As it turns out, estimations excluding the first five and a half years of the inflation series show that the media can lead the public agenda during periods of low inflation. Table 7.1 presents Granger exogeneity tests for a model using data from October 1991, a few months after the new inflation targets, to December 1995, the end of the time series. Note that during this time period, the CPI no longer had a significant impact on public opinion. Media content, on the other hand, exerted a significant influence, essentially replicating MacKuen and Coombs's findings (1981) and further demonstrating the important role of prominence in agenda-setting.

Table 7.1

Directions of causality: prominent issues during periods of low issue prominence

		Issue			
Variable		Inflation		Unemployment	
Dependent	Independent	χ^2	p	χ^2	p
Media	Media	3.169	(0.674)	**14.940**	**(0.002)**
	Public	**16.170**	**(0.006)**	**15.039**	**(0.002)**
	Policy	**12.902**	**(0.024)**	4.942	(0.176)
	Committees	–	–	1.472	(0.479)
	Bills	–	–	**8.644**	**(0.071)**
	Throne Speech	–	–	**114.268**	**(0.000)**
	Election	2.802	(0.423)	5.236	(0.155)
	Budget	**21.177**	**(0.000)**	**12.520**	**(0.006)**
	Real world	0.702	0.951	**25.390**	**(0.000)**
Public	Media	**11.152**	**(0.048)**	4.124	(0.248)
	Public	**69.203**	**(0.000)**	**521.787**	**(0.000)**
	Election	1.832	(0.608)	**20.324**	**(0.000)**
	Real world	4.094	(0.393)	3.997	(0.406)
Policy	Media	**10.171**	**(0.071)**	**29.183**	**(0.000)**
	Public	7.220	(0.205)	2.078	(0.556)
	Policy	0.816	(0.976)	**12.009**	**(0.007)**
	Committees	–	–	4.337	(0.114)
	Bills	–	–	2.289	(0.683)
	Throne Speech	–	–	**14.767**	**(0.001)**
	Budget	5.151	(0.161)	2.740	(0.434)
	Real world	**12.585**	**(0.013)**	5.313	(0.257)
Period		91:10 to 95:12		86:8 to 89:12	
Lags/df		3		3	

Note: Cells contain chi-square (χ^2) results, with p values in parentheses, from Granger causality tests based on a SUR estimation of equations 6.1 to 6.3, using monthly data from 1985 to 1995. Text in bold is significant at $p < .10$.

The situation for unemployment is not as clear-cut, but there is also evidence of a slightly increased media role during periods of low unemployment. Table 7.1 shows the Granger tests for a SUR model re-estimated for August 1986 to December 1989, a period of low and falling unemployment. In the policy equation, the significance of the real-world measure disappears and the media coefficients become statistically significant. This is an obvious and important change in the equation, and exactly what we would expect from decreased prominence. Predictors of the public agenda change in the same direction, but not so dramatically. The unemployment rate, formerly significant, no longer plays a leading role. The media agenda increases in strength and significance, but although the media agenda at lag 1 is statistically significant at $p = .08$, the summed coefficients for three lags are not strong enough to reject the null hypothesis of no significant effects.

The unemployment results are less pronounced, then, but are nevertheless another example of the relationship between prominence and the potential for media influence. In fact, it is striking that in both cases the roles of the media agenda and real-world indicators are virtually reversed. The results in Table 7.1 indicate that prominence plays an especially important role in agenda-setting. (For a similar test using UK data, see Soroka 2002b.) The impact of prominence is not only evident cross-sectionally, as prominent issues show weaker agenda-setting by the media, but also longitudinally, as media and real-world roles change over time with the relative prominence of issues.

The Duration of Issues: National Unity

The results for inflation and unemployment illustrate the importance of considering over-time changes in issue attributes when modelling agenda-setting dynamics. It follows that more than just changes in prominence should be considered. Other attributes can change, after all, and estimations might improve by taking this into account.

The attribute that most clearly changes over time, regardless of the issue, is duration. As discussed in Chapter 2, Zucker (1978) suggests that the age of an issue will affect the potential for media effects. A new issue, he proposes, is more open to media impact since the public knows little. As time progresses, the public learns more and is less susceptible to manipulation. Moreover, the public becomes bored. This is Downs's central hypothesis (1972) – issues will rise and fall over time in large part because the public has a limited attention span.

Testing this hypothesis depends in part on our ability to determine the beginning of an issue. The point at which an issue becomes "old" likely varies across issues and is more difficult to determine, but this is probably less important. Given a time period, one can simply drop cases from the end and watch for changing dynamics. The point at which a statistical model changes – provided it changes at all, and in the right direction – will likely be the dividing line between what Downs (1972, 39-40) calls "alarmed discovery and euphoric enthusiasm" and the "gradual decline of intense public interest."

That said, the starting point of an issue need not be pinpointed exactly; a rough estimate will probably suffice. An issue need not be entirely "new" either. A reframed issue or a new subissue will probably also have effects on agenda-setting dynamics. Indeed, this is the thrust behind much of the policy agenda-setting work dealing with problem definition and issue framing. Rochefort and Cobb (1994), for instance, note that describing an issue in a new way often wins attention. Baumgartner and Jones's work on air transportation policy (1994) and other issues (1993) offers evidence that a reframing of issues in the media or policy agendas is often associated with increased attention.

Following from this premise, national unity issues offer an opportunity to examine the effects of issue duration on agenda-setting. There is a strong argument that the national unity issues of the late 1980s were new and different from those that preceded them. There is little doubt that the 1982 patriation of the Constitution and the addition of the Charter of Rights and Freedoms fundamentally changed national unity issues in Canada. And if the events of the late 1980s were not directly a function of the new Constitution itself, they were certainly a product of Quebec's not having signed it (which created the need for the Meech and Charlottetown Accords). Thus, the period from 1985 to 1995 is a period of national unity debate distinctly different from that which preceded it.

Accordingly, the national unity model was re-estimated, dropping cases from the end and anticipating a change in causal relationships. The expectation was that national unity issues would be relatively "new" in 1985, and that public opinion would therefore follow media content. The situation would change in 1992, however, when public opinion would anticipate changes in the media and policy agendas, as national public attention was waning and the federal government was turning away from the business of accords. The Chapter 6 model suffered by including both periods in a single estimation. The result was a model in which each agenda affects the other, with the exception of the one causal link we expect the most: a policy impact on the media. Dropping the later period from the estimation should lead to clearer, and more policy-driven, results.

Table 7.2 presents Granger exogeneity tests for a period ending in March 1992, and offers a much more coherent picture of agenda-setting dynamics. First and most important, the public is no longer a significant predictor of either the media or policy agenda. Public opinion is led by the media, which in turn are driven by Question Period content, committee reports, and legislative initiatives. In truth, the media–Question Period relationship is a reciprocal one. Nevertheless, governmental issue dynamics are evident when the last three years – the period when national unity issues apparently grew "old" – are dropped from the analysis.

In sum, national unity results provide some evidence that duration is an important element in the agenda-setting process. The potential for media impact is limited by the age of an issue, although it is likely that a new issue frame, or new subissue, is just as good as an entirely new issue. In the case of national unity, the Meech Lake and Charlottetown Accords represented a new element in the national unity debate, and one for which the public responded to policy and media agendas. This lasted for only a short time, however, before the public, and the media and policymakers soon after, grew bored with the issue and moved on to other things.

Table 7.2

Directions of causality: national unity, before the Charlottetown Accord

		Issue	
Variable		National unity	
Dependent	Independent	χ^2	p
Media	Media	**28.672**	**(0.000)**
	Public	3.089	(0.378)
	Policy	**8.035**	**(0.045)**
	Committees	**11.164**	**(0.004)**
	Bills	**11.510**	**(0.021)**
	Throne Speech	0.222	(0.895)
	Election	1.914	(0.590)
	Budget	5.224	(0.156)
Public	Media	**13.896**	**(0.003)**
	Public	**96.875**	**(0.000)**
	Election	0.802	(0.849)
Policy	Media	**12.119**	**(0.007)**
	Public	4.923	(0.178)
	Policy	3.593	(0.309)
	Committees	0.995	(0.608)
	Bills	4.353	(0.360)
	Throne Speech	1.724	(0.422)
	Budget	5.637	(0.131)
Period		85:6 to 92:3	
Lags/df		3	

Note: Cells contain chi-square (χ^2) results, with p values in parentheses, from Granger causality tests based on a SUR estimation of equations 6.1 to 6.3, using monthly data from 1985 to 1995. Text in bold is significant at $p < .10$.

A Leading Newspaper?

A final way in which the Chapter 6 models might be changed is through the addition of other exogenous variables, either through breaking down the current variables or adding completely new ones. This is not to say that an unlimited number of variables should be added; describing as much of the variation as is possible with a limited number of variables is, after all, more convincing than a regression with an endless supply of independents. Nevertheless, there are several important exogenous variables that might both add to the predictive power of the equations and demonstrate an important element of the agenda-setting process. Environmental issues, for instance, might be driven by the interest-group agenda. We may also be able to more accurately measure media effects by either breaking down or adding to the media measure used earlier. This final topic is taken up next, as we focus attention on the possibility of a leading newspaper and the potential effects of taking this into consideration in the expanded estimations of the agenda-setting process.

It has often been suggested that the *New York Times* (*NYT*) plays a leading role among US newspapers. For instance, Gans (1979) notes that the *NYT* and the *Washington Post* are often used by editors as early indications of stories' newsworthiness, as does Miller (1978) in her study of the American press and congressmen. Reese and Danielian (1989) find empirical evidence of this phenomenon; they show that the *NYT* played a leading role in breaking the drug issue in the US.

Taras (1990) proposes a similar role for the *Globe and Mail* in Canada, suggesting that it helps set the agenda for other media. This view is buttressed by Fletcher's finding (1981) that a vast majority of media managers across Canada read the *Globe and Mail*. Evidence in column 2 of Table 3.1 (Chapter 3) also points to the possibility that the *Globe* stands apart from other Canadian newspapers. In three of eight cases – as many as *La Presse* – the *Globe* is the paper whose elimination leads to the highest alpha coefficient. This may be simply because the *Globe* is following a different agenda, but it may also be because it is setting the agenda and issue salience rises for this paper sooner than for the others. The evidence is not overwhelming, considering that the *Globe* stands out in only three of eight issues. The possibility that the *Globe* plays a leading role in Canada is worth exploring, however.

Alternatively, it may be that the Canadian equivalent of the *NYT* is the *NYT* itself. The *NYT* is, after all, a highly regarded newspaper with a global circulation. It is not unreasonable to suggest that media – newspapers and otherwise – outside the US see it in the same way as those in the US. And in Canada the potential for American influence appears to be especially strong.

Testing the influence of the *NYT* in Canada is of course a much larger issue than simply investigating the leading role of the *Globe and Mail*. The latter adds to our understanding of the relationship between Canadian newspapers; the former speaks to broader questions about domestic policymaking and international relations. Both investigations suggest how Chapter 6 models might be expanded, however, and this is the central focus of the analyses that follow.

The *Globe and Mail*

The potential effects of the *Globe and Mail* on other Canadian newspapers are tested here using the following autoregressive distributed lag (ADL) model:

$$Others_t = \alpha + \sum_{k=1}^{K} \beta_{1(k)} Others_{t-k} + \sum_{k=1}^{K} \beta_{2(k)} Globe_{t-k} + \varepsilon_t \qquad (7.1)$$

where *Globe* is the *Globe and Mail* time series for each issue, and *Others* is a measure made up of the remaining seven newspapers. Four lags ($k = 4$) of each variable are included, based on the assumption that any effects will have taken place within a four-week period. Four lags is also enough to eliminate any autocorrelation from the various models' residuals, and few enough to minimize problems with multicollinearity.

The significance of the *Globe* lags provides a test of the hypothesis that this paper leads other Canadian newspapers. Table 7.3 presents the results of the estimation of equation 7.1 for each issue. To conserve space, only the summed values for the lagged coefficients are displayed; the value for *Globe and Mail*, for instance, represents the value of all four lagged coefficients combined. The third column includes a Granger-style *F*-test, testing the null hypothesis that the cumulative impact of the lagged *Others* or *Globe* variables is equal to zero. Issues are listed by issue type, although no obvious trend in this regard is apparent.

Ignoring the bottom four rows for the time being, previous values for *Other* newspapers are the best predictors of the current values in all cases except inflation. Above and beyond this impact, the *Globe and Mail* is a significant predictor of other newspapers' emphasis for three issues: debt and deficit, inflation, and taxes. (These latter two series were ones in which the *Globe* stood apart in Table 3.1's alpha results.) Effects of the *Globe* for the other five issues are insignificant.

The national unity issue deserves some further analysis. Previous tests demonstrated that *La Presse* follows a different path from the English-language newspapers on national unity issues. This is in line with previous research emphasizing regional differences where national unity issues are concerned. Taking this into account, the test for a leading newspaper here is re-estimated in two ways in the bottom rows of Table 7.3. First, the possibility that *La Presse* leads English-language newspapers is tested. The poor

Table 7.3

The *Globe and Mail* as a leading newspaper

Issue	Independent variables	Dependent variable: Other newspapers$_t$		
		Summed lags	SE(β)	F-test[a]
Prominent issues				
Inflation	Others$_{t-1,4}$	0.191	(0.087)	11.256***
	Globe$_{t-1,4}$	1.694***	(0.475)	3.589**
Unemployment	Others$_{t-1,4}$	0.445***	(0.069)	14.406***
	Globe$_{t-1,4}$	-0.028	(0.680)	0.255
Sensational issues				
AIDS	Others$_{t-1,4}$	0.498***	(0.063)	20.960***
	Globe$_{t-1,4}$	0.483	(0.480)	0.488
Crime	Others$_{t-1,4}$	0.550***	(0.062)	21.679***
	Globe$_{t-1,4}$	0.338	(0.284)	1.199
Environment	Others$_{t-1,4}$	0.796***	(0.041)	95.277***
	Globe$_{t-1,4}$	0.393	(0.226)	1.572
Governmental issues				
Debt/deficit	Others$_{t-1,4}$	0.295***	(0.072)	5.127***
	Globe$_{t-1,4}$	1.650**	(0.522)	3.667**
Taxes	Others$_{t-1,4}$	0.857***	(0.032)	187.980***
	Globe$_{t-1,4}$	0.461*	(0.223)	3.948**
National unity	Others$_{t-1,4}$	0.800***	(0.039)	126.811***
	Globe$_{t-1,4}$	0.007	(0.180)	0.755
National unity[b]	Others$_{t-1,4}$	0.798***	(0.040)	103.676***
	La Presse$_{t-1,4}$	0.000	(0.047)	1.438
National unity[c]	Others$_{t-1,4}$	0.738***	(0.057)	44.695***
	Globe$_{t-1,4}$	0.186	(0.153)	0.224

Notes: Cells contain results from OLS regressions, using weekly data from 1985 to 1995.
[a] df = 4, 519.
[b] Including the *Globe and Mail* in Others.
[c] Excluding *La Presse* in Others.
* $p < .05$, ** $p < .01$, *** $p < .001$

coefficient for *La Presse* indicates that this is not the case – *La Presse* and the English-language newspapers are simply following different paths where national unity is concerned, although previous results demonstrate that the gap is not necessarily as wide as has been assumed.

Next, the possibility that the *Globe* leads English-language newspapers is tested. The relationship between the *Globe* and other newspapers is re-estimated in the last two rows, this time excluding *La Presse* from the *Other* category. Again, there is no major change in coefficients or significance. It is worth noting here, however, that, unlike the other tests, when this one is repeated with only three lags, the *Globe and Mail* F-test is significant ($F = 2.55431$, $p = .038$). There is a possibility, then, that the *Globe and Mail* leads English-language newspapers for national unity issues.

In sum, evidence suggests that the *Globe and Mail* sometimes plays the role of a leading newspaper in Canada, similar to the role of the *New York Times* in the US. Is there a pattern to when the *Globe* has or does not have an impact on other newspapers' agendas? One could argue that debt/deficit, inflation, national unity, and taxes are "national" issues, while crime, environment, and unemployment are more localized in nature. If this is true, it appears as though the *Globe* leads on "national" issues. This hypothesis requires further testing, however. It is not intuitively obvious that AIDS is a national or local issue, and convincingly categorizing the other issues requires more background research than is provided here. Nevertheless, Table 7.3 suggests that the *Globe* is sometimes a leading newspaper in Canada, and that further study might reveal a pattern to this newspaper's leading role.

These tests suggest that Chapter 6 models might be re-estimated separating the *Globe* from other newspapers. For inflation, debt/deficit, and taxes – issues for which the *Globe* plays a leading role – this may result in a more accurate model. Models are not re-estimated along these lines here, however. This section is just a beginning: considering the *Globe* on its own introduces the possibility that other papers might lead for other issues, and this possibility suggests a myriad of further tests and models. Nevertheless, the tests above indicate the potential for this line of analysis in the future. In the meantime they serve as a useful precursor to the next section, which investigates a leading newspaper whose potential effects are important enough to justify a more thorough analysis.

The *New York Times*

Hoberg (1991) examines the potential for cross-border agenda-setting in the policymaking arena, suggesting that Canadian environmental policy development has been influenced by US policies. Surprisingly, however, there is no agenda-setting research examining the interplay between two countries' media and public agendas. This is especially striking considering the Canadian context, where there is the widely recognized possibility that Canadian media and public agendas are affected by US media, either through direct media-public effects or through inter-media influence.

It is a simple enough process to collect US media data, compare them with Canadian media content, and add the time series to the Chapter 6 SUR estimations. Accordingly, data were collected for the four issues for which US media influence seemed most likely: AIDS, environment, inflation, and unemployment. Figure 7.1 displays the results, plotting the *NYT* time series against the Canadian media times series collected for the analysis in previous chapters.

Figure 7.1

Canadian and US media content, by issue

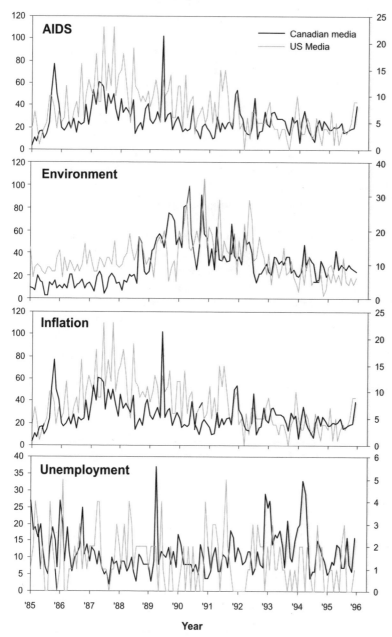

First, an ADL model similar to that for the *Globe and Mail* was estimated:

$$CDNnews_t = \alpha + \sum_{k=1}^{K} \beta_{1(k)} CDNnews_{t-k} + \sum_{k=1}^{K} \beta_{2(k)} NYT_{t-k} + \varepsilon_t \quad (7.2)$$

where *CDNnews* is the measure built from all eight Canadian newspapers, and *NYT* is the *New York Times* series. Again, the model includes four lags of each variable, and weekly series are used. Table 7.4 presents the results.

No causal effects are found for AIDS, environment, or unemployment. For inflation, however, there is evidence that US media content affects Canadian media content. It may be that the *NYT* is doing a good job of anticipating economic conditions – it could be serving here as a proxy for economic conditions rather than as an indication of the US media agenda. On the other hand, the media effects for inflation could be genuine; Canadian media attention to inflation could be driven in part by US media.

We can test this possibility more convincingly by adding the *NYT* variable to the Chapter 6 models, where most other variables and effects are controlled for. In fact, this is the case for all four issues: the possibility that the *NYT* affects any of the Canadian media, public, or policy agendas can be tested by adding *NYT* variables to the Chapter 6 SUR estimations. The models are re-estimated with these new variables, and results are presented in Table 7.5. Since most coefficients are unchanged by the addition of the US media variables, the table includes an abbreviated list of Granger exogeneity results.

For AIDS, environment, and unemployment, only the tests of US and Canadian media variables are listed. The latter are included since these are

Table 7.4

The *New York Times* as a leading newspaper

	Independent	Dependent variable: CDN newspapers$_t$		
Issue	variables	Summed lags	SE(β)	F-test[a]
AIDS	CDN Newspapers$_{t-1,4}$	0.473***	(0.065)	19.538***
	NYT$_{t-1,4}$	0.344	(0.214)	1.516
Environment	CDN Newspapers$_{t-1,4}$	0.808***	(0.041)	98.092***
	NYT$_{t-1,4}$	0.216	(0.138)	1.666
Inflation	CDN Newspapers$_{t-1,4}$	0.303***	(0.084)	13.658***
	NYT$_{t-1,4}$	0.252*	(0.120)	2.497*
Unemployment	CDN Newspapers$_{t-1,4}$	0.441***	(0.068)	13.342***
	NYT$_{t-1,4}$	-0.047	(0.349)	1.250

Notes: Cells contain results from OLS regressions, using weekly data from 1985 to 1995.
[a] df = 4,519
* $p < .05$, ** $p < .01$, *** $p < .001$

Table 7.5

US media influence on agenda-setting in Canada

Variable			Issue							
		AIDS		Environment		Unemployment		Inflation	
Dependent	Independent	χ^2	p	χ^2	p	χ^2	p	χ^2	p
CDN media	CDN media	2.285	(0.515)	7.029	(0.219)	**14.094**	**(0.003)**	**28.650**	**(0.000)**
	US media	**11.138**	**(0.011)**	**10.700**	**(0.058)**	3.513	(0.319)	**10.265**	**(0.068)**
	US CPI	–	–	–	–	–	–	2.605	(0.626)
Public	CDN media	2.478	(0.479)	1.614	(0.899)	1.962	(0.580)	2.484	(0.779)
	US media	0.969	(0.809)	**10.298**	**(0.067)**	4.659	(0.199)	**10.734**	**(0.056)**
	US CPI	–	–	–	–	–	–	**15.040**	**(0.005)**
Policy	CDN media	0.980	(0.806)	**12.804**	**(0.025)**	4.428	(0.219)	5.807	(0.325)
	US media	**8.777**	**(0.032)**	**13.872**	**(0.016)**	0.081	(0.994)	6.337	(0.275)
	US CPI	–	–	–	–	–	–	**10.406**	**(0.034)**
US media	US media	–	–	–	–	–	–	**42.539**	**(0.000)**
	US CPI	–	–	–	–	–	–	3.000	(0.558)
Lags/df		3		5		3		5	

Note: Cells contain chi-square (χ^2) results, with p values in parentheses, from Granger causality tests based on a SUR estimation of equations 6.1 to 6.3, with the addition of *NYT* variables, using monthly data from 1985 to 1995. Text in bold is significant at $p < .10$.

the variables most likely to change with the addition of the US variables. There is no change, however, in the significance of the Canadian media variables for AIDS or unemployment. For unemployment, in fact, there are no agenda-setting effects by the Canadian or US media. For AIDS, the US media leads both Canadian media and Question Period attention to this issue. There is evidence in Table 7.5, then, of a causal relationship. The assumption of causality seems a larger leap of faith when we start to consider agendas from outside Canada, but evidence in this direction suggests the importance of further investigation and the possibility of cross-border agenda-setting for AIDS.

The results for environment are more striking. In this case, the formerly significant effects of the Canadian media on the public agenda disappear, and are replaced by a stronger impact of the *NYT* on the Canadian public agenda. The policy agenda, on the other hand, is driven by both the Canadian and US media agendas. Again, the possibility that these are something other than causal relationships should be considered. It may be that it is not the *NYT* itself that is driving other agendas. This newspaper may simply be a more accurate surrogate of the general media agenda – newspaper, television, and radio – affecting the Canadian public. As with AIDS, however, evidence supporting the possibility of US media impact justifies further investigation.

The AIDS and environment estimations are similar in that both expanded models indicate US influence while the preceding ADL models of the media alone did not. This newfound US media influence could be a product of two modelling differences. First, the expanded models use monthly time series, whereas the previous models used weekly series. Changing the level of aggregation could alter the results, as could the more prolonged period taken into account in the new estimations. Second, evidence of US media influence could appear here because this second estimation controls for other influences – it is a more accurate model of the larger process.

The inflation estimation in Table 7.5 is different from the others in that it involves a more complex adjustment to the original Chapter 6 model. In this case, both the *NYT* and the US CPI are included in the model, using the same number of lags as the other variables. A fourth equation is also added, predicting present *NYT* content as a function of past *NYT* content and the US CPI.

The results in the final columns of Table 7.5 indicate that, even controlling for the US inflation rate, attention to inflation in the *NYT* affects Canadian media and public concern about this issue. Canadian media respond to the *NYT*; the Canadian public responds to both the *NYT* and the US CPI; Canadian policymakers respond to the US CPI. There is a logic to these results. Based on previous results, for instance, we would expect the media to be the least correlated with real-world indicators. There is also some logic in the fact that while the Canadian media and public are affected by the *NYT*, policymakers are led only by real-world indicators from the US. These suppositions are secondary, however. The most important finding here is simply that changes in media and public attention in Canada are related to *NYT* content above and beyond any relationship with the US CPI.

As with environment, the explanation that the *NYT* simply acts as a better indication of the overall media agenda than the measure based on Canadian newspapers is appealing. On the other hand, the idea that US attention to inflation drives Canadian attention is not entirely unlikely: the two countries' economies are linked, and important economic news in the US often receives considerable Canadian coverage. Of the issues surveyed here, the results for inflation offer the strongest evidence of the potential importance of US media in Canadian agenda-setting dynamics, and confirm the potential for this type of cross-border agenda-setting analysis.

Summary and Conclusions

This chapter has demonstrated that the Chapter 6 models can be further refined, and that our picture of the agenda-setting process can improve as a result. For prominent issues, evidence for inflation and unemployment shows that it is worth examining changes in prominence over time as well as across issues. For sensational and governmental issues, issue duration appears to affect agenda-setting dynamics. National unity results show that the potential for public agenda-setting was limited after the 1992 referendum; moreover, in contrast to the results in Chapter 6, these results display the predicted governmental-issue dynamics when we consider the pre-1992 period. Finally, this chapter points to the value of considering cross-border agenda-setting influences. The US media agenda is a prime candidate for Canadian agenda-setting studies, and examples above point to the possibility of agenda-setting effects by the US media for AIDS, environment, and inflation.

What do this chapter's results mean for the Chapter 6 models? The results from Chapter 6 are accurate, specifically for the 1985-95 time period but also generally speaking. This chapter's results make two important additions to the Chapter 6 conclusions, however. First, adding variables above and beyond the three main agendas can add valuable detail to agenda-setting models. Models based on the media, public, and policy agendas cover substantial territory, and the dynamics identified in these models are most often robust enough to remain unchanged as other variables are added. Nevertheless, more comprehensive models can lead to more nuanced results.

Second, results indicate that issue attributes can change over time, and agenda-setting dynamics can change as a result. For instance, the complex Chapter 6 results for national unity appear to have been the function of a time period that spanned two distinctly different phases in issue dynamics. When the periods were separated, the underlying dynamics became much clearer. Similarly, inflation and unemployment estimations indicate that investigating media effects for prominent issues should involve a consideration of changes in the relative salience of real-world indicators. Results for these issues indicate that agenda-setting analyses concerned with causality and issue attributes might often be best served by the two-stage method of investigation used here. Initially, all available data can be used and the predominant issue dynamics will often, although not always, emerge. As a second step, breaking the time period into parts may help identify changes in causal dynamics related to variation in issue prominence and duration.

8
Final Conclusions

> The existence of an agenda-setting function of the mass media is not *proved* by the correlation reported here, of course, but the evidence is in line with the conditions that must exist if agenda-setting by the mass media does occur.
>
> – Maxwell E. McCombs and Donald L. Shaw (1972, 184)

McCombs and Shaw were appropriately conservative in their conclusions. They relied on a relatively small body of data and assumed rather than tested directions of causality. Nevertheless, their evidence was convincing enough to generate decades of agenda-setting analyses. It started the ball rolling, and the resulting body of literature provides strong evidence of the original Chapel Hill hypothesis.

The current research has sought to build on this accumulated evidence, testing a wide range of agenda-setting hypotheses and combining a number of agenda-setting literatures. The selection of introductory passages drawn largely from agenda-setting studies speaks to the space the current study seeks to fill. This work is presented to a great extent as a culmination of past aggregate-level agenda-setting research. It seeks to justify the framework, and to combine and learn from past public opinion- and policy-centred agenda-setting analyses. In doing so, an expanded model and issue typology have been presented as means of reconciling diverse findings. Moreover, they have been offered as guides to current and future analyses. Examples in previous chapters demonstrate the value of the expanded agenda-setting framework and the threefold issue typology, and indicate the means by which agendas can be measured and the framework practically applied.

The preceding analyses have sought to cover a wide range of related hypotheses. For the most part, specific findings have been reviewed along the way. This final chapter briefly reconsiders the results and discusses how they relate to each other and the general contributions that they, as a group, make to agenda-setting analysis in general and individual studies of media, public opinion, and policymaking in particular. The chapter begins with a concise review of findings and closes with a general discussion of the expanded agenda-setting framework.

Summary of Findings

About Agenda-Setting

A central goal of the preceding analyses has been to demonstrate the value of an agenda-setting framework. The sheer volume of agenda-setting literature offers considerable proof of its merit, but the fact that various subfields remain disjointed and empirical work is often poorly conceived has tended not to help agenda-setting's case. The work presented here represents an attempt to solve some of the conceptual and methodological difficulties that exist in agenda-setting research, and proving the value of an agenda-setting framework is an important part of this.

The biggest advantage of an agenda-setting framework is its ability to combine mass media research, the study of public opinion, and public policy analysis. Each of these fields is important in its own right. They are clearly inter-related, however, and agenda-setting provides a vernacular facilitating directly comparable hypotheses and measures. Consequently, an agenda-setting framework permits the incorporation of the three fields into a single, more complete, and more precise form of empirical analyses. Unfortunately, this has seldom been the case. Except for a few recent studies, the vast majority of agenda-setting analyses have concentrated on one or two agendas, ignoring other relationships fundamental to an accurate picture of issue dynamics. The public and policy agenda-setting literatures have for the most part remained isolated. This book attempts to ameliorate this division and thereby improve agenda-setting modelling.

Moreover, the expanded agenda-setting model described in Chapter 1 goes some way towards suggesting a means by which empirical models should be conceived and estimated. The initial attraction of agenda-setting for many theorists was that the framework lent itself to empirical analysis. Thus, an effort to more explicitly link agenda-setting with an appropriate empirical model represents an important development.

About Canadian Agendas

Despite work that emphasizes regional differences, there is a Canadian newspaper agenda. This is true when we consider issue salience, at least. It is likely that a more context-sensitive study would find more significant differences between newspapers, but where simple agenda-setting is the primary focus, it is clear that the assumption of a Canadian newspaper agenda is on firm ground. Evidence presented here certainly does not identify any trends based on region or ownership. The only trend identified is based on issue salience: increased issue salience leads to increased inter-newspaper consistency. It is likely, therefore, that agenda-setting by the media is doubly strengthened during periods of high salience, because of both the increase in salience and the increased similarity in media content.

There is also a Canadian public agenda. Again, there is undoubtedly more regional difference in issue opinions than in the rather thin measure of public opinion used here. Where issue salience is concerned, however, there is a considerable degree of inter-regional consistency, albeit stronger longitudinally than cross-sectionally. While issue salience in provinces tends to rise and fall at the same time, the mean level of concern varies across provinces. Evidence indicates that this difference is partly attributable to variations in real-world conditions: provinces in which concern tends to be higher also tend to be those where real-world conditions are more prominent. Audience attributes also play a role. Concern for national unity, for instance, is highest in regions with large francophone populations. This is not a groundbreaking finding, but it points to the value of agenda-setting studies that are better equipped to investigate the relationship between individual-level variables and agenda-setting effects.

While evidence tends to support the existence and measurability of the media and public agendas, the policy agenda is quite a different story. There are a wide variety of possible measures, certainly, even in a system of government decidedly less open than that of the United States. Those examined in this book include Question Period content, legislative initiatives (both government and private member's bills), committee reports and activities, and Throne Speech content. The fact most obvious in the analysis, however, is that these measures are often only tangentially related. In short, government attention to issues can take a wide variety of forms and can take place in many venues. A Question Period measure can be interpreted only as a measure of Question Period; a measure of legislative initiatives measures nothing other than legislative initiatives. Accordingly, government attention must be measured at a number of levels, and these should be included individually in empirical analysis. Yearly analyses might find more success in tracking general policy trends using a single series. For monthly or weekly analysis, however, multiple measures are required.

About the Agenda-Setting Process

Agenda-setting dynamics are often multidirectional. Media and policy agendas often interact, for instance, each affecting the other as issues rise and fall in significance. It is incorrect to assume, as much past work has done, that the media agenda leads the public agenda. In some circumstances, the public will affect the media agenda, and models of agenda-setting effects will often need to take this possibility into account.

It is also true that the direction of effects changes across issues, and information on issue attributes can help predict the directions of influence that are most likely. The three issue types proposed here – prominent, sensational, and governmental – have proven useful in this regard. Generally speaking, a given issue at a given time will display either prominent-, sensational-, or governmental-issue dynamics. In the first case, real-world indicators will lead the media, public, and policy agendas. In fact, the obtrusiveness or prominence of issues is perhaps the most powerful predictor of the presence or lack of agenda-setting dynamics. Issues that are more prominent will show smaller agenda-setting effects, and the evidence in this book demonstrates that both inflation and unemployment are prominent issues. Furthermore, as the degree of prominence changes over time, so too will the potential for agenda-setting dynamics. Tests have found evidence that in periods of low unemployment or inflation, there is greater opportunity for media effects.

Sensational issues, on the other hand, will tend to be media-driven. These issues are recognizable in that they will generally not be obtrusive, allowing for the possibility of media effects. They will probably, but not necessarily, lend themselves to dramatic events. Environment proved to be a good example of such an issue, demonstrating the power of media to affect both public and policy agendas.

Debt/deficit offered the clearest example of governmental-issue dynamics – a policy agenda that leads the media and public agendas. National unity and taxes were other examples, although the results for these issues were less clear-cut. It is significant that the national unity results were clarified when a shorter time period was used. This example proved not only the importance of issue duration but also the possibility that issue types can vary over time. Over an extended time period, issues can exhibit a number of different dynamics, and the national unity estimation proved the value of reconsidering the time period under investigation.

It is true that the three issue types used here are not mutually exclusive, nor are they entirely well equipped to be predictive rather than just descriptive. It will not always be obvious that an issue is sensational as opposed to governmental, for instance, before agenda-setting effects are estimated. In many cases, however, prior consideration of issue attributes will suggest hypotheses about how an issue will move between agendas, and demonstrating this was a primary goal of the tests of issue types in this study. In the future identifying empirical measures of issue attributes that allow for a more accurate and well-founded prior classification of issues might be a worthwhile endeavour. In the meantime it is clear that the strength and direction of agenda-setting dynamics vary across issues and over time, that these variations are directly linked to issue attributes, and that the various attributes are reasonably well summarized by the prominent/sensational/governmental issue typology.

Finally, it is worth noting that additional variables can be added to the agenda-setting models proposed here. Chapter 7 included a preliminary test of the US media agenda, but this is by no means the only possibility. Dearing (1989) considers the polling agenda; Kaye (1994) examines the agendas of political parties. The interest group agenda represents another option worth exploring, especially for environmental issues. Models of the expanded agenda-setting process will improve in both accuracy and explanatory power as additional agendas are included in future analyses.

In Closing

Politics and political science are too often divided. Political science has a value on it own, certainly, but efforts to link academic work with everyday politics are especially valuable. To a large extent, agenda-setting research represents one such effort.

Much of the work described in this book dwells on an agenda-setting framework's ability to combine work from a variety of political science subfields. It is also true, however, and perhaps more significant, that agenda-setting links these research streams with the stuff of everyday politics. Issues are a central feature of day-to-day political interactions; they are the primary unit of analysis in newscasts, in Question Period, in discussions between friends, and also in agenda-setting research. As a result, not only does agenda-setting analysis provide an empirical means of testing various theories of media effects and policymaking but its results tell the real-world history of an issue. Agenda-setting work thus serves both academic and pragmatic purposes: it tests political science hypotheses but also provides sensible explanations of how issues rise and fall and how politics functions in a society.

The story of how politics functions is complicated, to be sure. Despite considerable efforts to build a relatively simple model, the evidence presented here suggests that an accurate picture of political communications in Canada is necessarily complex. Nevertheless, this work can be distilled into a few short conclusions. The interactions between media, public, and policymakers can be understood in terms of issue dynamics, or the rise and fall of issue salience over time. Causal relationships between the three major agendas are often multidirectional. An order to the interactions can be detected, however: issue dynamics change systematically based on issue attributes, which vary both across issues and over time. It follows that an understanding of issue attributes, the measurement of agendas, and the various relationships between them provides us with the tools to model and better understand political communications, policy development, and everyday politics.

Appendix A:
Time Series Methods and Agenda-Setting

> The cross-sectional sample survey favored by most researchers
> is hardly a powerful means of testing a dynamic process such as
> agenda-setting. A more appropriate strategy is to search for media
> effects over time, as news coverage and public concern evolve.
>
> – Roy L. Behr and Shanto Iyengar (1985, 39)

The chapters of this book outline the considerable methodological variance that exists between agenda-setting studies. Agendas have been operationalized in many different ways, and real-world indicators have not always been included. Perhaps the area in which the most inter-study variance exists is statistical methodology. One of the original attractions of agenda-setting, particularly for public opinion analysts, was the fact that it was well suited to empirical analysis. The appropriate statistical method has rarely been clear, however, and this lack of methodological clarity has grown as both agenda-setting models and econometrics have become more sophisticated. Both fields have reached a stage where more advanced and reliable analyses are possible.

This appendix describes the statistical methods used in the preceding chapters. Its goal is to justify the modelling methods used in Chapters 6 and 7. The by-product is a discussion of time series methods in general, with specific reference to their use in agenda-setting research.

This appendix relies on a wide variety of statistical sources. Where necessary, individual sources are cited. On a more general level, the texts that provided the background for the following section should be noted. Furthermore, since the current review seeks only to provide a concise background to the statistical procedures used, the following may prove useful for those interested in more detailed information. The two most widely used texts, both for general and time series information, were Judge et al. 1988 and Kennedy 1998. For more specific information on particular topics, see the following: general time series information – Catalano et al. 1983, Chatfield 1989, Harvey 1981, and Hendry 1995; ARIMA analysis – Box and Jenkins 1976, Box and Pierce 1970, Hoff 1983, and McCleary and Hay 1980; Granger causality – Freeman 1983 and Granger 1969. All estimations were performed with RATS (Regression Analysis for Time Series), and the accompanying texts (Doan 1996; Enders 1996) are also useful in describing most time series techniques.

The Advantages and Disadvantages of Time Series Data

Time series data have advantages and disadvantages. The greatest single advantage, as reflected in the quotation at the beginning of this appendix, is that they permit better tests of causality than do cross-sectional data – they are better suited for testing dynamic processes. Their greatest disadvantage is that they violate a number of assumptions central to the statistical techniques most common in political science.

The use of time series data is further confused by the fact that choosing a statistical strategy is rarely straightforward. Most often several methods can be used, and the choice (and justification) of a particular method is left to the researcher. Unfortunately, many political science analyses, and agenda-setting investigations in particular, suffer from either poor technical choice or inadequate description of the methods used.

This appendix represents one effort to avoid these problems. The discussion begins with a brief description of the time series methods most common in recent agenda-setting research: cross-correlation functions (CCFs) and ARIMA modelling. This description is also used as an introduction to the general statistical problems of time series data. Following from the suggestion that neither CCFs nor ARIMA modelling is the best method for exploring agenda-setting, autoregressive distributed lag (ADL) models, Granger causality, and seemingly unrelated regressions (SUR) are described. These methods are increasingly used in political science and political communications analyses, and they provide estimation procedures that are especially functional for the agenda-setting research in the preceding chapters.

The discussion of time series methods that follows is far from comprehensive and is not intended to replace the need for statistics texts. Rather, it offers a guide to some time series methods used or useful in agenda-setting analysis. A major difficulty with interpreting past work is the lack of a straightforward description not only of the techniques used but also of the connections between the various techniques. This discussion of time series strategies emphasizes ways in which various methods are linked, and indicates when each has been used and when each is appropriate. The review should help not just in describing the preceding analyses but also in interpreting past work and in pointing to the methodological links between this and previous agenda-setting studies.

Cross-Correlation Functions (CCFs)

The most common method of searching for bivariate time series relationships is through cross-correlation functions (CCFs) – correlation coefficients calculated between two series at various lags and leads. The equation is identical to that for a regular correlation coefficient (see any statistics text), with the subscript for the variables changed to reflect their time series structure. In agenda-setting studies with monthly data, CCFs are generally calculated for from 12 to 15 lags and leads, with the expectation that effects have occurred within that many months. Results are in the form of a series of correlation coefficients: y_t and x_t, y_t and x_{t-1}, y_t and x_{t-2}, and so on.

The interpretation of CCFs is relatively straightforward. If there are statistically significant correlations, there is probably a relationship between the two series, and the lags and leads for which significant correlations exist are thought to give an indication of causality. If a media series at time t–1 is significantly correlated with a public opinion series at time t, for instance, there is reason to believe that the media series leads the public opinion series. This has been the premise behind the large number of agenda-setting studies relying on CCFs for evidence of effects (e.g., Ader 1995; Smith 1987; Wanta et al. 1989).

Although CCFs can be a useful indication of bivariate relationships, they should be regarded as only a very weak indicator of causality. Perhaps more fundamentally, the calculation of confidence intervals for CCFs will not always be reliable. An accurate confidence interval is dependent on the mean for the residuals (error term) being equal to zero, and on there being no serial correlation in the residuals (see Kennedy 1998). These assumptions are difficult to meet with time series data, where there is frequently a trend and where the value for the current period *(t)* is often related to the value at the previous period *(t–1)*. The heteroskedasticity and serial correlation that result have no direct impact on the correlation coefficients themselves, but they do bias confidence intervals and significance tests.

Pre-Whitening with ARIMA Models

In an effort to avoid the difficulties noted above, some recent agenda-setting analyses have turned to ARIMA modelling (e.g., Gonzenbach 1992, 1996; Hester and Gonzenbach 1995; Rogers et al. 1991; Soroka 1999a, 2000; Zhu et al. 1993). The function of an ARIMA model can be described in both statistical and conceptual terms. Conceptually speaking, its purpose is to separate the regular behaviour of the series from the white-noise component. "Regular behavior includes trends and cycles that remain relatively constant over time as well as behavior in which an event at one point in time has a predictable effect on a limited number of subsequent values" (Catalano et al. 1983, 510). An ARIMA model, properly specified, accounts for this regular behaviour. The residuals, or white noise, from the ARIMA model represent the true movements in the series: the series' behaviour above and beyond its regular trends and cycles. This white noise most often contains the information pertinent to the analysis of the relationships between time series. Following from this premise, Gonzenbach (1996) and others use ARIMA modelling to pre-whiten their series and then search for relationships using CCFs, without the problems of autocorrelation and trend. (Gonzenbach is a clear advocate of the use of ARIMA modelling in agenda-setting work. Above and beyond his own analyses, see Gonzenbach and McGavin's description [1997] of agenda-setting methodologies.)

Statistically speaking, ARIMA models help solve the problems of time series data by purging the series of trend and serial correlation. This is the central statistical purpose of ARIMA analysis in agenda-setting work: to transform the data and create a series free of serial correlation and trend. Specifying the actual ARIMA model is a complicated procedure, involving a combination of preliminary diagnostic tests and subsequent testing of residuals. The details of the Box-Jenkins method are well described elsewhere (e.g., Harvey 1981; Hoff 1983; McCleary and Hay 1980) and need not be reviewed here. It is worth noting, however, that the vast majority of time series in political communications work tend to be relatively simple to fit. Generally speaking, these time series tend to exhibit limited autocorrelation in the form of impacts declining gradually over time.

Unfortunately, ARIMA pre-whitening may have adverse effects on subsequent analyses. There is no absolutely correct ARIMA model for a time series; we can do our best at selecting a model, but we can rarely be sure that the model is doing exactly what we want it to do. Specifically, while we can test the residuals for trend and autocorrelation to be sure these problems do not remain, we cannot be sure that the model is purging the series of autocorrelation and trend without affecting other dynamics.

As a result, we might be "throwing the baby out with the bath water" (Durr 1993, 164): an ARIMA model might model out autocorrelation and trend in a given time series, along with some more fundamental dynamics. This is particularly the case when differencing is used (Freeman et al. 1998, 1,295; Sims 1980). Moreover, ARIMA pre-whitening might also affect the relationship between two series. Two different ARIMA models or the unequal effects of the same model on two different time series might affect the existence or timing of the correlation between those two series (Catalano et al. 1983, 512).

These concerns have been expressed in some recent agenda-setting work. For instance, Blood and Phillips (1997, 98) note that conventional procedures call for pre-whitening "at the cost of losing valuable information and at the risk of wrongly determining the existence or absence of agenda-setting effects between series comprised of filtered or manipulated data" (see also Feige and Pearce 1979). As a result, it is worth considering whether pre-whitening is necessary, or whether we can find a way to use the original series. It is often preferable to do the latter. The choice of statistical methods in the current work is based on this hypothesis, in line with some recent work in political science and econometrics (e.g., Freeman 1983; King 1989). The benefits and disadvantages of pre-whitening continue to be debated.

Autoregressive Distributed Lag (ADL) Models

The following sections describe a number of related statistical methods: Direct Granger tests, vector autoregression, and seemingly unrelated regressions. These are all variations on the general autoregressive distributed lag (ADL) model, a relatively simple regression model that includes, as the name suggests, both autoregressive and distributed lag components. The general ADL model is as follows:

$$y_t = \alpha + \sum_{k=1}^{K} \beta_{1(k)} y_{t-k} + \sum_{m=1}^{M} \beta_{2(m)} x_{(1)t-m} + \sum_{p=1}^{P} \beta_{3(p)} x_{(2)t-p} + \dots \varepsilon_t \quad \text{(A.1)}$$

where k, m, and p are the number of lags, and y_t and x_t are time series variables. Essentially, y_t is a function of past values of itself, and past values of a series of other variables. Note that both the number of these independent variables and the number of lags can vary.

A major advantage of ADL models where this work is concerned is that they can be used with autocorrelated variables. So long as the number of lagged values of the variables accounts for their autocorrelation, the estimation will remain unbiased (provided that the time series are stationary and that the autocorrelation can be accounted for by the simple AR processes). (For more information on stationarity, see Hendry 1995 or most recent econometrics texts; for information on AR processes versus other forms of autocorrelation, see the previous section, on ARIMA models.)

The number of lags in an ADL model should be based on a combination of theoretical consideration and the need to account for autocorrelation. If there is reason to believe that effects will occur within a four-month period, for instance, four lags (of monthly data) should be used. Provided these lags are enough to account for the autocorrelation in the various series, this model is appropriate. Whether autocorrelation is accounted for can be tested by checking the model's residuals for autocorrelation using one of several statistics, including the Ljung-Box Q-statistic, Durbin's m, or the Lagrange multiplier (LM) test (see Judge et al. 1988; Dezhbakhsh 1990; Breusch 1978; Godfrey 1978; Chatfield 1989; Ljung and Box 1978; for instances of their use in agenda-setting work, see Cohen 1995 and Hill 1998).

Provided an ADL model passes the test for autocorrelation (and often multicollinearity, since many ADL models will include a large number of lagged variables), it can provide a useful and relatively simple means of examining causal relationships between time series variables. On its own, an ADL model does not test the direction of causality, however. When we select a single variable as the dependent, we simply assume causality. In some cases this is justified, and a simple ADL model is suitable. (For a discussion on choosing a strategy based on knowledge of causality, see Catalano et al. 1983.) In other cases, when causality is unclear, other ADL-based methods are more appropriate.

The Direct Granger Method

Following Freeman (1983), the term "Direct Granger method" is used here to refer to a test for Granger causality between two variables – direct in the sense that it is a single-stage method, requiring no pre-whitening. This is the first advantage of the Direct Granger method: like the preceding ADL models, the Direct Granger equations include past values of both series. Estimates can remain unbiased in spite of autocorrelated time series data, and the process can proceed without pre-whitening.

Several agenda-setting analyses have combined ARIMA modelling and Granger causality (e.g., Gonzenbach 1996; Soroka 1999a). This is probably unnecessary, however. As mentioned earlier, if the number of lags used in the Granger causality model is enough to account for the series' autocorrelation (and the series include only simple AR processes), no pre-whitening should be required. Freeman (1983) makes a direct comparison of pre-whitening and the Direct Granger technique, and finds that the latter method offered a more accurate test of causality than ARIMA modelling followed by causality tests. The Direct Granger tests described below provide one possible means of testing causal links between autocorrelated time series without worrying about pre-whitening.

The second advantage of the Direct Granger method is that it provides a much stronger indication of causality than CCFs. Granger causality is based on the notion that "Y_t is causing X_t if we are better able to predict X_t using all information than if the information apart from Y_t had been used" (Granger 1969, 428). This is assessed based on the following ADL equations, representing relatively simple causal models of the time series x_t and y_t:

$$x_t = \alpha_1 + \sum_{k=1}^{K} \beta_{1(k)} x_{t-k} + \sum_{k=1}^{K} \beta_{2(k)} y_{t-k} + \varepsilon_{1t} \tag{A.2}$$

$$y_t = \alpha_2 + \sum_{k=1}^{K} \beta_{3(k)} x_{t-k} + \sum_{k=1}^{K} \beta_{4(k)} y_{t-k} + \varepsilon_{2t} \tag{A.3}$$

where k is the number of lags used in the estimation, and $\varepsilon_{1t}/\varepsilon_{2t}$ are randomly distributed and uncorrelated error terms.

A Direct Granger test involves estimating equations A.2 and A.3 with and without the independent variable. Equation A.2, for instance, is estimated excluding and including y_{t-k}. An F- or chi-square (χ^2) test is then used to test the null hypothesis that the history of this independent makes no significant contribution to the current value of the dependent above and beyond the contribution of past values of the dependent. If the unrestricted version is considerably better, the F-test is significant and we can conclude that the independent variable in this equation "Granger-causes" the other. This process is performed for equations A.2 *and* A.3, allowing for four possibilities: (1) there is a one-way causal relationship; (2) there is "feedback," or reciprocal causal relationship; (3) there is an instantaneous causal link; and (4) there is no relationship between the variables (Granger 1969).

The decision as to how many lagged coefficients of the series should be used in a Direct Granger test is important. First, the models' residuals should be checked for autocorrelation – the models will have to include at least as many lags as required to avoid autocorrelated residuals. A further consideration is that the direction of causality can sometimes change if different numbers of lags are used. The most common case is one in which the direction of causality is confused because too few lags are used. The most conservative course of action is to test for Granger causality several times, using different numbers of lags. This allows us to both (1) check whether the direction of causality remains the same when different numbers of lags are used, and (2) identify the number of lags that produces the strongest effect.

The use of Granger causality tests in political science has increased in recent years, and several agenda-setting studies use Direct Granger testing to test or establish causality (e.g., Bartels 1996; Brosius and Kepplinger 1990; Smith 1987). The preceding chapters rely intermittently on Granger causality tests, either by using the Direct Granger approach as described above or by adapting the test to models including additional independent variables. The method by which the equations are estimated, however, requires further discussion.

Seemingly Unrelated Regressions (SUR)

The preceding description assumes that the Direct Granger equations (A.2 and A.3) can be solved individually. As a corollary, it ignores the possibility that the models are theoretically and empirically linked. There is often reason to believe that they are, however. From a theoretical standpoint, the individual regressions are components of a larger agenda-setting process. Statistically speaking, it is likely that equations A.2 and A.3 will have correlated error terms. If this is the case, an estimation procedure that takes this correlation into account will yield more accurate estimates.

The objective, then, should often be to solve the equations as a system, and there are several methods to do this. Vector autogression (VAR) is one example, and is ideally used to solve a system of equations for which the independent variables are the same. (For a description of VAR, see Sims 1980; for an example of their use in political science, see Hartley and Russett 1992 or Bartels 1996.)

When the independent variables are different, a Zellner-Aitken seemingly unrelated regressions (SUR) estimation (1962) is more appropriate. (For more information on the situations in which SUR estimations are appropriate, see Zellner 1962, 351; Dwivedi and Srivastava 1978; and Greene 1992, 488-89). SUR techniques use Aitken's generalized least squares (GLS) to solve a system of equations accounting for linked error terms, often leading to more efficient estimates than either ordinary least squares (OLS) on individual equations or a VAR estimation. "Essentially, this gain in efficiency occurs because in estimating the coefficients of a single equation, the Aitken procedure takes account of zero restrictions on coefficients occurring in other equations" (Zellner 1962, 353).

SUR estimation techniques have been used in political science, although not in agenda-setting work (Chappell 1990; Chappell and Suzuki 1993; Chubb 1985; Ferejohn and Calvert 1984; Freeman 1983; Hoole and Huang 1992; Simon et al. 1991). Because the models of the expanded agenda-setting process described in Chapters 6 and 7 are based on a three-equation system in which the independent variables for each equation are different, they rely on a SUR estimation.

Presenting SUR Results

Multiple lags, multicollinearity, and an estimation that allows for both direct and indirect effects combine to make the interpretation of VAR or SUR models considerably more difficult than that of a standard regression. Bartels's agenda-setting work (1996) is a typical example of the use of VAR methodology, and provides a telling illustration of the resulting difficulties in interpretation (see also Enders and Sandler 1993 and MacKuen et al. 1992). Bartels examines the reciprocal relationship between the US press and politicians, estimating causal relationships between the *New York Times,* local newspapers, ABC News, executive branch activities, and congressional activities. Five equations are estimated, one for each variable and all of which have seven lags of all five variables as predictors. This results in a very large number of coefficients that on their own are hard to interpret. Moreover, multicollinearity probably precludes examining the individual coefficients, since it produces the possibility that, while the overall effects are accurate, the individual coefficients are not.

Freeman et al. (1989) discuss these difficulties with VAR, suggesting that, compared with regular structural equation modelling, VAR sacrifices quantitative precision for better accuracy in causal inference. We can no longer examine individual coefficients, but we can make more convincing claims about causal relationships between variables. As the preceding discussion indicates, these claims are not made by interpreting individual coefficients. Rather, as Bartels (1996) demonstrates, hypotheses are tested using Granger exogeneity tests and impulse response functions.

Granger exogeneity tests are used to test the null hypothesis that the sum of all lags for a given variable in a single equation is equal to zero. This is an extension of the Granger causality test described earlier. In this case, a multivariate model is estimated with and without one of the independent variables (y_t). The two models are compared, and an F- or chi-square test is used to test the null hypothesis that the history of y_t contributes nothing to the prediction of x_t. As described earlier, a statistically significant test is taken as an indication of causality, while an insignificant test is taken as an indication that y_t is exogenous to the process. These tests do not indicate the sign of the effects, however, and negative effects do exist sometimes. Accordingly, an additional method of interpreting the results is required.

Impulse response functions – part of a class of interpretive methods referred to as innovation accounting – are a common method of interpreting VARs and are also applicable to SUR estimations. This method provides information on both the direction and duration of effects, information lacking in the Granger tests. The mechanics of impulse response functions are complicated and will be left to statistics texts (e.g., Enders 1996). A very brief explanation here will suffice. All autoregressive (AR) processes have a moving average (MA) representation, where each endogenous variable is expressed in terms of present and past values of shocks to each endogenous variable. For a VAR/SUR estimation, the resulting sets of MA coefficients are called impulse response functions, and plotting them over time is a way to visually represent the behaviour of the endogenous series in response to shocks in one of these series. If results are standardized, the effects of or on each of the variables are directly comparable, and provide a useful tool with which to examine the magnitude, direction, and duration of agenda-setting dynamics.

The central difficulty with this method is that a typical VAR or SUR model is under-identified, so a researcher must impose additional restrictions in order to identify the MA coefficients and plot impulse response functions. Nevertheless, impulse response functions are one of the few means by which the results of a VAR or SUR model can be intelligently interpreted, and the graphic display of impulse responses is especially attractive to those interested in dynamic effects.

A major task of the researcher, then, is to decide which restrictions should be imposed: essentially, which variables should be allowed to affect each other contemporaneously at period 1, and which should affect each other only after period 1. This decision is made somewhat easier when the model, like the ones used here, already includes several restrictions. A totally unrestricted VAR, after all, offers no clue as to which restrictions should be imposed for innovation accounting, while a SUR model already suggests several restrictions.

The two most common methods of imposing restrictions – of decomposition – are the Choleski and Bernanke/Sims decompositions. The method proposed by Sims (1986) and Bernanke (1986) is more flexible, and more appropriate for the current analyses, where the following restrictions, written in matrix notation, seem the most appropriate:

$$\begin{bmatrix} e_{1t} \\ e_{2t} \\ e_{3t} \end{bmatrix} = \begin{bmatrix} 1 & 0 & 0 \\ 0 & 1 & 0 \\ 0 & 0 & 1 \end{bmatrix} \begin{bmatrix} \varepsilon_{1t} \\ \varepsilon_{2t} \\ \varepsilon_{3t} \end{bmatrix} \tag{A.4}$$

for a three-variable system, where variables 1 to 3 are media, public, and policy; and where e are the models' residuals, ε are the innovations, 1 implies the possibility of contemporaneous effects, and 0 implies a contemporaneous correlation restricted to 0. Taken in total, the decomposition used here allows each series to affect itself contemporaneously, while effects on other agendas take one period to manifest themselves.

Impulse response functions used in Chapter 6, then, are plotted using this Bernanke/Sims decomposition as it is estimated by RATS. These results should be recognized as the product of a slightly different system from the original equations. They nevertheless provide useful information about inter-agenda dynamics, and are used along with the Granger exogeneity tests to describe such dynamics.

A Note on Stationarity in Time Series Econometrics

A variable is said to be stationary when the mean and variance remain constant over time. A recent development in econometrics has been the recognition that many economic time series are nonstationary, and that using normal econometric methods with these variables can present considerable difficulties. Confidence intervals and R^2s, for instance, can be biased in such a way that researchers are more likely to reject the null hypothesis. A considerable amount of recent work has been dedicated towards dealing with this difficulty (e.g., Hendry 1986). Methods of solving the nonstationarity problem remain contentious, however, and it is not always clear, both to users of econometrics and econometricians themselves, how one should identify and deal with nonstationary variables.

Identifying nonstationarity is a difficult task. It normally takes the form of testing for a unit root, a coefficient of 1 for an AR process, which indicates that innovations have a permanent impact on the time series. The identification of a unit root is difficult, however, since AR coefficients are biased downward in cases where a unit root exists. Specific unit roots tests have been developed, the number and scope of which are far too great to summarize adequately here. Maddala and Kim (1998) provide a thorough review, the thrust of which is that (1) the most common unit root tests lack power and should not be used, and (2) it is rarely clear when other unit root tests are appropriate.

If and when nonstationary variables are identified, they can be dealt with in several ways (Maddala and Kim 1998, 20-29). Typically, difference-stationary variables, showing a change in variance over time, can be differenced as in the Box-Jenkins ARIMA modelling procedure. Trend-stationary variables, showing a change in mean over time, can be accommodated by including a time variable in the regression equation. Both these methods may result in lost information, however, as has been noted in the preceding discussion of ARIMA modelling. There are a number of other alternatives. Co-integration analysis and error correction models (ECM) are two methods specifically oriented towards working with nonstationary data. Unfortunately, neither lends itself to the type of analysis required here. Freeman et al. (1998) examined the difficulties created for VAR estimations by nonstationary time series variables, and suggested a new method of estimation (FM-VAR); this method has seen little use, however.

Turning to the analyses in Chapters 6 and 7, preliminary testing showed that real-world indicators often exhibited nonstationarity and tested positive for unit roots. Before their use in the SUR models, however, these series were differenced. This was due less to a concern about unit roots than to a belief that the public reacts to changes in, rather than the absolute value of, real-world indicators such as the CPI, crime rates, number of AIDS cases, or unemployment rate. Nevertheless, the differencing meant that the problems with nonstationarity in these series were largely avoided.

A variety of preliminary tests were conducted for the remaining series. Policy and media series almost always tested negative for a unit root, while some public opinion series tested positive, probably partly a function of using linear interpolation to fill in missing data in the monthly series. In the estimations, however, the potential effects of nonstationarity in these series were ignored. This decision was in line with many advocates of VAR/ SUR methodologies (see, for instance, Doan 1996), and was based here on three factors in particular. First, a review of unit root tests, as described above, did not indicate that unit root tests were consistently reliable. Second, if unit roots were found, no method of dealing with them was readily available, at least not one that did not risk a loss of information. Finally, some econometricians have charged that "there are serious conceptual difficulties in distinguishing unit root processes from stationary processes in finite samples" (Campbell and Perron 1991, 2). Ten years of data is a relatively small sample by econometric standards, and so these concerns are certainly applicable here. In sum, then, while this note serves to warn the reader about the potential problems with nonstationarity, the analyses above only partly deal with these difficulties.

A Note on Causality in Time Series Econometrics

The term "causality" is used frequently in this book; it is the central focus of agenda-setting research, and testing it is the major goal of a natural history inquiry. Econometric definitions of causality are firmly rooted in Granger's notion of causality (1969): *x* causes *y* if past values of *x* help predict current values of *y*. Related in part to Granger's work, Charemza and Deadman (1997, 165) provide a succinct statement of the three assumptions underlying econometric notions of causality:

1 "Instantaneous causation" does not exist, since there is always a time difference between independent actions.
2 For similar reasons, there is no such thing as "simultaneous causation."
3 The future cannot "cause" the present.

The last element is the most important, and points to the fact that what econometricians call a causal relationship is most often more closely related to temporal precedence than it is to proof of actual causation.

"It must be stressed at the outset that this [econometric] notion of causality is a purely statistical one, and it does not correspond to any acceptable definition of cause and effect in the philosophical sense" (Harvey 1981, 301; see also Darnell 1994). Rather, indicators of causality in this work, and in econometric analyses in general, are based on the assumption that causality and predictability are interchangeable, at least empirically speaking. Of course, this problem is most damaging for analyses in which there is no strong theoretical justification for the hypothesized causal relationship. This is not the case here, where a combination of intuition, practical experience, and accumulated empirical evidence suggests that relationships between the media, the public, and policymakers are in fact causal. This work assumes, then, that proof that one variable predicts – or "Granger-causes" – another is adequate proof of causation.

Summary

Past longitudinal agenda-setting work has relied on a variety of statistical methods, not all of which are appropriate for either time series data or demonstrations of causality. This appendix has noted that CCFs provide a weak indication of causality and that their significance tests are most often biased due to the nature of time series data. Pre-whitening the data using ARIMA modelling is one way to solve this problem, but this risks losing important information. An alternative, and the one suggested here, is to use ADL models that can account for the serial correlation in time series data and thereby offer accurate estimates and confidence intervals without pre-whitening, at least when the data are the product of relatively simple AR processes.

VAR and SUR are essentially extensions of the simple ADL model, and are increasingly used in political science analyses using time series data. By solving a set of equations as a system, these methods offer the possibility of more accurate coefficient estimates when equations are related. The models in Chapters 6 and 7 are best estimated by Zellner's SUR; accordingly, this is the predominant method of estimation in this work. Because the estimations result in a large number of coefficients and allow for both direct and indirect effects, interpreting the coefficients themselves is difficult. Consequently, two additional methods of interpretation are used: Granger exogeneity tests and innovation accounting.

This appendix has also noted the difficulties surrounding both non-stationarity and notions of causality in econometrics. Regarding nonstationarity, our review acknowledges that unit roots are a potential problem, but the estimations that follow go only some way towards dealing with this difficulty. Regarding causality, econometric definitions of causality are reviewed, and the assumptions that underlie the following work in this regard are clarified. In short, our causality tests are based on temporal precedence – a reasonable supposition considering the strength of arguments concerning, and accumulated evidence of, causal relationships between the media, public, and policy agendas.

Appendix B:
The Media Agenda

All media time series are the product of title searches using the keywords listed below. For the sake of brevity, plural forms of words are not listed although they were always included in the search where appropriate. The same applies to the feminine version of French keywords. When individual words could not be used as search terms on their own, other words were added to the search (e.g., AIDS). The results of all searches were verified manually, and unrelated articles were deleted when identified.

AIDS
English: AIDS and HIV, AIDS and health, AIDS and epidemic, AIDS and death, AIDS and treatment, AIDS and research, AIDS and drug, AIDS and medicine, AIDS and virus, AIDS and clinic, AIDS policy; *French: SIDA.*

Crime
English: crime, criminal, murder, murderer, rape, rapist, robbery, robber, theft, thief; *French: crime, criminel, meurtre, meurtrier, rapt, vol, voleur.*

Debt/Deficit
English: debt and national, debt and federal, debt and government, debt and public, deficit and national, deficit and federal; *French: dette* and *nationale, dette* and *fédérale, dette* and *gouvernement, dette* and *publique, déficit* and *national, déficit* and *fédéral.*

Environment
English: environment, environmental, environmentalist, environmentalism, conservation, conservationist, ozone, endangered and species, endangered and animal, endangered and plant, endangered and tree, endangered and fish, global warming, clearcut, clearcutting, acid rain, pollution, pollute, pollutant, polluter; *French: environnement, environnemental, environnementaliste, environnementalisme, conservation, conservationaliste, ozone, menacées* and

espèces, menacé and *animal, menacée* and *plante, menacé* and *arbre, menacé* and *poisson, réchauffement planétaire, coupe à blanc, pluies acides, pollution, polluer, polluant.*

Inflation
English: inflation; *French: inflation.*

National Unity
English: national unity, constitution, constitutional; *French: unité* and *nationale, constitution, constitutionnel.*

Taxes
English: tax and federal, GST; *French: impôt* or *taxe* and *fédérale, TPS.*

Unemployment
English: unemployment; *French: chômage.*

Appendix C:
The Public Agenda

This appendix includes both descriptive and diagnostic information on the public agenda time series. Coding schemes for the open-ended "most important problem" (MIP) question varied among polling organizations. The first section lists the codes used for each subject analyzed in the current work. The second lists the various surveys used from each polling firm, and the MIP question wording. A final section then discusses the problems with using different polling firms and compares results from the firms used here.

Wording and coding changes might lead to different MIP results across polling firms, but preliminary tests indicated a relatively high degree of consistency across polling firms. This is in line with work by Smith (1980, 1985), who suggests that wording changes for the MIP question in the US produce no significant changes in results. Nevertheless, this author's own work (Soroka 2001) suggests that differences across polling firms do exist. Using these data, "house effects" were not evident. For more detailed information on how wording, coding, and the number of responses can affect MIP results, the reader should refer to Soroka (2001).

MIP Coding Schemes

AIDS
Environics: AIDS; Pollara: AIDS.

Crime
Angus Reid: crime/capital punishment/gangs; CBC: crime or violence; Environics: crime/law and order; Pollara: crime/violence.

Debt/Deficit
Angus Reid: deficit/government spending; CBC: national debt/deficit; Decima: deficit; Environics: deficit/public debt, government spending/waste; Pollara: deficit/government spending, high deficit/debt.

Environment
Angus Reid: environment/pollution; CBC: acid rain, pollution/environmental problems; Decima: environment; Environics: pollution/environment, ecology/energy; Gallup: environment/pollution; Pollara: environment.

Inflation
CBC: high cost of living/high prices; Decima: inflation; Environics: cost of living/inflation; Pollara: inflation/cost of living.

National Unity
Angus Reid: national unity/Quebec, constitution/Meech Lake, language issues; CBC: language, Meech Lake Accord, Quebec, unity/national unity; Decima: national unity; Environics: French/English problems, Meech Lake/constitution, national unity, Quebec separating; Gallup: constitution/national unity; Pollara: constitution, national unity/separation.

Taxes
Angus Reid: taxes/tax reform/GST; CBC: GST/new sales tax, over-taxation (income/sales tax), taxes (unspecified); Decima: government/taxes; Environics: GST, taxes (not including GST), taxes/income taxes; Gallup: GST/taxes; Pollara: taxes, high taxes

Unemployment
Angus Reid: unemployment/jobs; CBC: unemployment/lack of jobs; Decima: unemployment; Environics: unemployment; Gallup: unemployment; Pollara: unemployment/jobs.

Survey Information

Angus Reid
Question: To begin with, thinking of the issues presently confronting Canada, which one do you feel should receive the greatest attention from Canada's leaders? What other issues do you think are important for Canada right now?
Polls: 1993: January, March, May, July, September, November; 1994: January, March, May, July, September, November, December; 1995: January, March, May, July, September, November.

CBC/Globe and Mail
Question: What would you say is the most important problem facing Canada today? [What would you say is the next most important problem facing Canada today?]
Polls: 1989: October; 1990: June/July, October; 1991: April.

Decima

Question: In your opinion, what is the most important problem facing Canada today – in other words, the one that concerns you personally the most?

Polls: 1985: March, June, September, December; 1986: March, June, September, December; 1987: March, June, September, December; 1988: March, June, September, December; 1989: March, June, September, December; 1990: March, June, September, December; 1991: March, June, September, December; 1992: March, June, September, December; 1993: March, June, September, December; 1994: February, May, August, November; 1995: February. (Decima changed their data collection methods in 1994. While field dates for the previous polls took place in the months indicated, the field dates for the 1994 and 1995 polls spanned each quarterly period. The middle month of the field work is used as the date for these last few polls.)

Environics

Question: In your opinion, what is the most important problem facing Canadians today?

Polls: 1985: April; 1986: February; 1987: March; 1988: February, May, October, December; 1989: March, June, October, December; 1990: March, June, October; 1991: January, April, July, October; 1992: February, May, August, November; 1994: March, June, September, December; 1995: March, June, September, December.

Gallup

Question: What do you think is the most important problem facing this country today?

Polls: 1985: June; 1986: June; 1987: February; 1988: February, July; 1990: January; 1995: January.

Pollara

Question: In your opinion, what is the single most important problem facing this country today?

Polls: 1992: January, April, August, November; 1993: February, May, August, October; 1994: February, May, August, November; 1995: February, May, August, November.

Appendix D:
The Policy Agenda

Hansard and Throne Speech content analysis and legislation counts were performed manually, and did not use specific keywords. Although government spending was not used in the final agenda-setting models, time series data were collected for preliminary analyses. The sources of these government spending data are noted below.

AIDS
Includes all AIDS-related expenditures made through the Department of Health and Welfare. Included, for instance, is all money spent on education and prevention, biomedical initiatives, care, treatment and support, support to nongovernmental organizations, coordination and collaboration costs, the Aboriginal AIDS Program, administration and support, and the AIDS secretariat.

> *Sources:* 1983-93: Evert A. Lindquist and David M. Rayside, "Federal AIDS Policy for the 1990s: Is It Too Early for 'Mainstreaming' in Canada?" in *How Ottawa Spends: The Politics of Competitiveness, 1992-1993,* ed. Francis Abele (Ottawa: Carleton University Press, 1992), pp. 313-52; 1993-1995: figures are taken from the Canadian Strategy on HIV/AIDS, Phase II.

Crime
Based on the amount of money spent each year on the "Protection of Persons and Property" (as defined by the National Tax Foundation) by the Solicitor General's department and the Department of Justice. Solicitor General responsibilities include the Canadian Security Intelligence Service (CSIS), the Correction Service, the office of the Correctional Investigator, the National Parole Board, the RCMP, and the RCMP external review committee and public complaints committee. The Department of Justice expenditures include the Canadian Human Rights Commission, the Supreme Court, the Federal Court, the Tax Court, the Commissioner for Federal Judicial Affairs, etc.

> *Source: The National Finances,* Canadian Tax Foundation, various years.

Environment
Based on the cash spent by the Department of the Environment on the Environmental Protection Service, Atmospheric Environment Service, Environmental Conservation Service, and Administration, as well as "other" environmental expenditures as classified in *The National Finances,* including expenditures made by Indian Affairs and Northern Development, Canada Mortgage and Housing Corporation (CMHC), and the National Capital Commission.

National Unity
The national unity data include a number of series:

(1) All cash spent by the Secretary of State (until 1994) or the Department of Canadian Heritage (1994 onward) on "Bilingualism Development" (as defined by the Canadian Tax Foundation). This includes the Official Languages Program, which deals with the promotion and use of official languages, as well as summer language bursaries.

(2) Expenditures on "Recreation and Culture" (as defined by the Canadian Tax Foundation), including postal subsidies, Canada Council, Telefilm Canada, National Archives, museums, Parks Canada, Fitness and Amateur Sport Program, National Capital Commission, and so on. Depending on the year, most of these expenditures were made through the Department of Canadian Heritage, the Secretary of State, or the Department of Communications.

Source: The National Finances, Canadian Tax Foundation, various years.

Unemployment
The series for unemployment is based on the expenditures on "Labour and Employment" (as defined by the National Tax Foundation). The series includes all expenditures on employment-related developmental uses programs, including such things as the Canada Employment Centres, the Work-Sharing Program, and job creation and training courses. Most expenditures were made through the Canada Employment and Immigration Commission (CEIC), although some expenditures in select years were made through the Department of Labour or the Department of Agriculture.

Source: The National Finances, Canadian Tax Foundation, various years.

Appendix E:
Real-World Indicators

Where possible, real-world indicators were collected for each issue. In most cases, more real-world indicators were collected than were used in the final agenda-setting models. All indicators and their sources are listed below.

AIDS
Number of reported cases of AIDS, all ages, Canada; reported yearly, divided into monthly increments.
> Source: Division of HIV/AIDS Surveillance, Bureau of HIV/AIDS, DTD, and TD, Laboratory Centre for Disease Control, Health Protection Branch, Health Canada, HIV and AIDS in Canada: Surveillance Report to December 31st, 1997 (April 1998), Table 10, p. 16.

Crime
Violent crime rate and % change in rate (1); property crime rate and change in rate (2); total police reported crime (excluding traffic offences) rate and change in rate (3).
> Source: Canadian Centre for Justice Statistics, Canadian Crime Statistics 1997, Statistics Canada, 1997, p. 14.

Debt/Deficit
Gross federal government debt (national debt), in millions, reported annually as of March 31 (1); federal government revenue and expenditure, in millions, reported annually as of March 31: Total Revenue (2) – Total Expenditure (3); debt, as a proportion of GDP = (1)/gross domestic product at market prices, expenditure-based, not seasonally adjusted, in millions (4); deficit, as a proportion of federal government revenue = [(2) – (3)]/(2).
> Sources: Statistics Canada – (1) CANSIM D469409; (2) CANSIM D464223; (3) CANSIM 464264; (4) CANSIM D15689.

Environment

Timber harvest levels: annual area harvested, thousands of hectares (1); new supplies of ozone-depleting substances (ODS), chlorofluorocarbons (CFCs) and other ODS (2); carbon dioxide emissions from fossil fuel use, in megatonnes (3); cumulative change in risked species, of all species, subspecies, and populations evaluated by the Committee on the Status of Endangered Wildlife in Canada (COSEWIC) (4); leading indicators for Canada/composite index of 10 indicators, unsmoothed (81 = 100); monthly change in composite index = $(5)_t - (5)_{t-1}$.

Sources: All sources are reported in Canada's Environmental Indicators Series from Environment Canada, but originate from the following sources: (1) Natural Resources Canada, Canadian Forestry Service, National Forestry Database; (2) Commercial Chemicals, Evaluation Branch, Environmental Protection Service, and Statistics Canada; (3) Environmental Protection Service, Environment Canada, and Statistics Canada; (4) COSEWIC Secretariat, Canadian Wildlife Service, Environment Canada; (5) CANSIM D100030.

Inflation

Consumer price indexes for Canada, monthly, 1996 classification (1992 = 100, all items) (1); monthly change in CPI = $(1)_t - (1)_{t-1}$; leading indicators for Canada/composite index of 10 indicators, unsmoothed (81 = 100) (2); monthly change in composite index = $(2)_t - (2)_{t-1}$.

Sources: (1) CANSIM P100000; (2) CANSIM D100030.

Taxes

Income tax burden = income taxes (1)/GDP (6); personal tax burden = personal taxes (2)/(6); consumption tax burden = consumption taxes (3)/(6); general sales tax burden = general sales taxes (4)/(6); total tax burden = (1) + (3) + misc. taxes (5)/(6).

Sources: (1) CANSIM D464225; (2) CANSIM D464226; (3) CANSIM D464229; (4) CANSIM D464230; (5) CANSIM D464237; (6) CANSIM 15689.

Unemployment

Unemployment rate for those aged 15 and over, reported monthly, unadjusted (1); change in unadjusted unemployment rate = $(1)_t - (1)_{t-1}$; unemployment rate for those aged 15 and over, reported monthly, seasonally adjusted (2); change in adjusted unemployment rate = $(2)_t - (2)_{t-1}$; leading indicators for Canada/composite index of 10 indicators, unsmoothed (81 = 100) (3); monthly change in composite index = $(3)_t - (3)_{t-1}$.

Sources: (1) CANSIM D980404; (2) CANSIM D980745; (3) CANSIM D100030.

References

Ader, Christine R. 1995. A Longitudinal Study of Agenda Setting for the Issue of Environmental Pollution. *Journalism and Mass Communication Quarterly* 72(2): 300-11.

Altheide, David L. 1991. The Impact of Television News Formats on Social Policy. *Journal of Broadcasting and Electronic Media* 35(1): 3-21.

–. 1997. The News Media, the Problem Frame, and the Production of Fear. *Sociological Quarterly* 38(4): 647-68.

Altheide, David L., and R. Sam Michalowski. 1999. Fear in the News: A Discourse of Control. *Sociological Quarterly* 40(3): 475-504.

Anderson, Alison. 1991. Source Strategies and the Communication of Environmental Affairs. *Media, Culture and Society* 13(4): 459-76.

Andrade, Lydia, and Garry Young. 1996. Presidential Agenda Setting: Influences on the Emphasis of Foreign Policy. *Political Research Quarterly* 49: 591-605.

Atwater, T., M.B. Salwen, and R.B. Anderson. 1985. Media Agenda-Setting with Environmental Issues. *Journalism Quarterly* 62: 393-97.

Bagdikian, Ben. 1987. *The Media Monopoly.* 2nd ed. Boston: Beacon Press.

Ball-Rokeach, Sandra J., and M.L. DeFleur. 1976. A Dependency Model of Mass Media Effects. *Communication Research* 3: 3-21.

Bartels, Larry M. 1996. Politicians and the Press: Who Leads, Who Follows? Paper presented at the Annual Meeting of the American Political Science Association, September, San Francisco.

Bartels, Larry M., and Henry E. Brady. 1993. The State of Quantitative Political Methodology. In *Political Science: The State of the Discipline II,* edited by Ada W. Finifter. Washington, DC: American Political Science Association.

Baumgartner, Frank R., and Bryan D. Jones. 1993. *Agendas and Instability in American Politics.* Chicago: University of Chicago Press.

–. 1994. Attention, Boundary Effects, and Large-Scale Policy Change in Air Transportation Policy. In *The Politics of Problem Definition: Shaping the Policy Agenda,* edited by David A. Rochefort and Roger W. Cobb. Lawrence: University Press of Kansas.

Behr, Roy L., and Shanto Iyengar. 1985. Television News, Real-World Cues, and Changes in the Public Agenda. *Public Opinion Quarterly* 49(1): 38-57.

Benton, Marc, and Jean P. Frazier. 1976. The Agenda-Setting Function of the Media at Three Levels of Analysis. *Communication Research* 3: 261-74.

Berkowitz, Dan. 1992. Who Sets the Media Agenda? The Ability of Policymakers to Determine News Decisions. In *Public Opinion, the Press, and Public Policy,* edited by J. David Kennamer. London: Praeger.

Bernanke, B. 1986. Alternative Explanations of the Money-Income Correlation. *Carnegie-Rochester Conference Series on Public Policy* 25: 49-100.

Birkland, Thomas A. 1997. *After Disaster: Agenda Setting, Public Policy, and Focusing Events.* Washington, DC: Georgetown University Press.

Blais, André, Blake Donald, and Stéphane Dion. 1996. Do Parties Make a Difference? A Reappraisal. *American Journal of Political Science* 40(2): 514-20.

Blake, Donald E. 1999. Economic Context and Public Opinion: The Case of Environmental Issues. Paper presented at Annual General Meeting of the Canadian Political Science Association, June, Sherbrooke, QC.

Blood, Deborah J., and Peter C.B. Phillips. 1997. Economic Headline News on the Agenda: New Approaches to Understanding Causes and Effects. In *Communication and Democracy: Exploring the Intellectual Frontiers in Agenda-Setting Theory,* edited by Maxwell McCombs, Donald L. Shaw, and David Weaver. Mahwah, NJ: Lawrence Erlbaum Associates.

–. 1995. Recession Headline News, Consumer Sentiment, the State of the Economy and US Presidential Popularity: A Time Series Analysis 1989-1993. *International Journal of Public Opinion Research* 7(1): 2-22.

Box, G.E.P., and G.M. Jenkins. 1976. *Time Series Analysis: Forecasting and Control.* San Francisco: Holden-Day.

Box, G.E.P., and David Pierce. 1970. Distribution of Residual Autocorrelations in Autoregressive-Integrated Moving Average Time Series Models. *Journal of the American Statistical Association* 65(332): 1509-26.

Breuning, Marijke. 1994. Belgium's Foreign Assistance: Decision Maker Rhetoric and Policy Behavior. *Res Publica* 36(1): 1-21.

Breusch, T.S. 1978. Testing for Autocorrelation in Dynamic Linear Models. *Australian Economic Papers* 17: 334-55.

Brosius, Hans-Bernd, and Hans Mathias Kepplinger. 1990. The Agenda-Setting Function of Television News: Static and Dynamic Views. *Communication Research* 17(2): 183-211.

–. 1992a. Beyond Agenda-Setting: The Influence of Partisanship and Television Reporting on the Electorate's Voting Intentions. *Journalism-Quarterly* 69(4): 893-901.

–. 1992b. Linear and Nonlinear Models of Agenda-Setting in Television. *Journal of Broadcasting and Electronic Media* 36: 5-23.

–. 1995. Killer and Victim Issues: Issue Competition in the Agenda-Setting Process of German Television. *International Journal of Public Opinion Research* 7(3): 211-31.

Brown, Michael, and John May. 1989. *The Greenpeace Story.* Scarborough, ON: Prentice Hall.

Bruce, Jean. 1966. A Content Analysis of Thirty Canadian Daily Newspapers Published During the Period January 1 – March 31, 1965, with a Comparative Study of Newspapers Published in 1960 and 1955. Report presented to the Royal Commission on Bilingualism and Biculturalism.

Cameron, David R. 1978. The Expansion of the Public Economy: A Comparative Analysis. *American Political Science Review* 72: 1243-61.

–. 1986. The Growth of Government Spending: The Canadian Experience in Comparative Perspective. In *State and Society: Canada in Comparative Perspective,* edited by Keith Banting. Toronto: University of Toronto Press.

Campbell, John Y., and Pierre Perron. 1991. Pitfalls and Opportunities: What Macroeconomists Should Know About Unit Roots. Paper presented at the National Bureau of Economic Research Macroeconomics Conference, March, Cambridge, MA.

Carmines, Edward G., and Richard A. Zeller. 1979. *Reliability and Validity Assessment.* Beverly Hills, CA: Sage Publications.

Carragee, Kevin, Mark Rosenblatt, and Gene Michaud. 1987. Agenda-Setting Research: A Critique and Theoretical Alternative. In *Culture and Communication: Methodology, Behavior, Artifacts, and Institutions,* vol. 3, edited by Sari Thomas. Norwood, NJ: Ablex Publishing.

Carroll, Raymond L., C.A. Tuggle, James F. McCollum, Michael A. Mitrook, Kevin J. Arlington, and John M. Hoerner Jr. 1997. Consonance in Local Television News Program Content: An Examination of Intermarket Diversity. *Journal of Broadcasting and Electronic Media* 41: 132-44.

Catalano, Ralph A., David Dooley, and Robert Jackson. 1983. Selecting a Time Series Strategy. *Psychological Bulletin* 94(3): 506-23.

Chappell, Henry W. Jr. 1990. Economic Performance, Voting, and Political Support: A Unified Approach. *Review of Economics and Statistics* 72: 313-20.

Chappell, Henry W. Jr., and Motoshi Suzuki. 1993. Aggregate Vote Functions for the US Presidency, Senate, and House. *Journal of Politics* 55(1): 207-27.

Charemza, Wojciech W., and Derek F. Deadman. 1997. *New Directions in Econometric Practice: General to Specific Modeling, Cointegration, and Vector Autoregression.* 2nd ed. Cheltenham, UK: Edward Elgar.

Chatfield, C. 1989. *The Analysis of Time Series.* London: Chapman and Hall.

Chiricos, Ted, Sarah Eschholz, and Marc Gertz. 1997. Crime, News and Fear of Crime: Toward an Identification of Audience Effects. *Social Problems* 44(3): 342-57.

Chubb, John E. 1985. The Political Economy of Federalism. *American Political Science Review* 79(4): 994-1015.

Cloutier, Edouard, Jean H. Guay, and Daniel Latouche. 1992. *Le virage: l'évolution de l'opinion publique au Québec depuis 1960, ou comment le Québec est devenu souverainiste.* Montreal: Québec/Amérique.

Cobb, R.W., and C.D. Elder. 1971. The Politics of Agenda-Building: An Alternative Perspective for Modern Democratic Theory. *Journal of Politics* 33: 892-915.

-. 1972. *Participation in American Politics: The Dynamics of Agenda Building.* Boston: Allyn and Bacon.

Cobb, Roger W., and Marc Howard Ross, eds. 1997. *Cultural Strategies of Agenda Denial: Avoidance, Attack, and Redefinition.* Lawrence: University Press of Kansas.

Cohen, Bernard C. 1963. *The Press and Foreign Policy.* Princeton, NJ: Princeton University Press.

Cohen, Jeffrey E. 1999. *Presidential Responsiveness and Public Policy-Making: The Public and the Policies that Presidents Choose.* Ann Arbor: University of Michigan Press.

-. 1995. Presidential Rhetoric and the Public Agenda. *American Journal of Political Science* 39(1): 87-107.

Cook, Fay Lomax, Tom R. Tyler, Edward G. Goetz, Margaret T. Gordon, David Protess, Donna R. Leff, and Harvey L. Molotch. 1983. Media and Agenda Setting: Effects on the Public, Interest Group Leaders, Policy Makers, and Policy. *Public Opinion Quarterly* 47(1): 16-35.

Cook, Timothy E. 1988. Press Secretaries and Media Strategies in the House of Representatives: Deciding Whom to Pursue. *American Journal of Political Science* 33(4): 1047-69.

Coulson, David C. 1994. The Impact of Ownership on Newspaper Quality. *Journalism Quarterly* 71(2): 403-10.

Crimmins, James E., and Paul Nesbitt-Larking. 1996. Canadian Prime Ministers in the House of Commons: Patterns of Intervention. *Journal of Legislative Studies* 2(3): 145-71.

Cronbach, L.J. 1951. Coefficient Alpha and the Internal Structure of Tests. *Psychometrika* 16: 297-334.

Danielian, Lucig H., and Stephen D. Reese. 1989. A Closer Look at Intermedia Influences on Agenda Setting: The Cocaine Issue of 1986. In *Communication Campaigns About Drugs: Government, Media, and the Public,* edited by Pamela J. Shoemaker. Hillsdale, NJ: Lawrence Erlbaum Associates.

Darnell, A.C. 1994. *A Dictionary of Econometrics.* Aldershot, UK: Edward Elgar.

Davie, William R., and Jung Sook Lee. 1995. Sex, Violence, and Consonance/Differentiation: An Analysis of Local TV News Values. *Journalism and Mass Communication Quarterly* 72(1): 128-38.

Dearing, James W. 1989. Setting the Polling Agenda for the Issue of AIDS. *Public Opinion Quarterly* 53: 309-29.

Dearing, James W., and Everett M. Rogers. 1996. *Agenda Setting.* Thousand Oaks, CA: Sage Publications.

DeGeorge, William F. 1981. Conceptualization and Measurement of Audience Agenda. In *Mass Communication Review Yearbook,* vol. 2, edited by G. Cleveland Wilhoit and Harold de Bock. Beverly Hills, CA: Sage Publications.

Demers, David Pearce, Dennis Craff, Yang-Ho Choi, and Beth M. Pession. 1989. Issue Obtrusiveness and the Agenda-Setting Effects of National Network News. *Communication Research* 16: 793-812.

Desveaux, James A., Evert A. Lindquist, and Glen Toner. 1994. Organizing for Policy Innovation in Public Bureaucracy: AIDS, Energy, and Environmental Policy in Canada. *Canadian Journal of Political Science* 27(3): 493-528.

Dezhbakhsh, Hashem. 1990. The Inappropriate Use of Serial Correlation Tests in Dynamic Linear Models. *Review of Economics and Statistics* 72(1): 126-32.

Diskin, Abraham, and Itzhak Galnoor. 1990. Political Distances Between Knesset Members and Coalition Behavior: The Peace Agreements with Egypt. *Political Studies* 38(4): 710-17.

Ditton, Jason, and James Duffy. 1983. Bias in the Newspaper Reporting of Crime News. *British Journal of Criminology* 23(2): 159-65.

Doan, Thomas A. 1996. *RATS User's Manual, Version 4*. Evanston, IL: Estima.

Docherty, David C. 1997. *Mr. Smith Goes to Ottawa: Life in the House of Commons*. Vancouver: University of British Columbia Press.

Dodge, David A. 1998. Reflections on the Role of Fiscal Policy: The Doug Purvis Memorial Lecture. *Canadian Public Policy* 24(3): 275-90.

Downs, Anthony. 1972. Up and Down with Ecology: The "Issue Attention Cycle." *The Public Interest* 28: 38-50.

Durr, Robert H. 1993. What Moves Policy Sentiment? *American Political Science Review* 87(1): 158-70.

Durr, Robert H., John B. Gilmour, and Christina Wolbrecht. 1997. Explaining Congressional Approval. *American Journal of Political Science* 41(1): 175-207.

Dwivedi, T.D., and V.K. Srivastava. 1978. Optimality of Least Squares in the Seemingly Unrelated Regression Equation Model. *Journal of Econometrics* 7(3): 391-95.

Eaton, H. 1989. Agenda-Setting with Biweekly Data on Content of Three National Media. *Journalism Quarterly* 66: 942-49.

Einsiedel, Edna F., Kandice L. Salamone, and Frederick P. Schneider. 1984. Crime: Effects of Media Exposure and Personal Experience on Issue Salience. *Journalism Quarterly* 61: 131-36.

Elkin, Frederick. 1975. Communications Media and Identity Formation in Canada. In *Communications in Canadian Society*, 2nd ed., edited by Benjamin D. Singer. Toronto: Copp Clark.

Elkins, David J. 1980. The Sense of Place. In *Small Worlds: Provinces and Parties in Canadian Political Life*, edited by David J. Elkins and Richard Simeon. Toronto: Methuen.

Enders, Walter. 1996. *RATS Handbook for Econometric Time Series*. New York: John Wiley and Sons.

Enders, Walter, and Todd Sandler. 1993. The Effectiveness of Antiterrorism Policies: A Vector-Autoregression-Intervention Analysis. *American Political Science Review* 87(4): 829-44.

Erbring, Lutz, Edie N. Goldenberg, and Arthur H. Miller. 1980. Front-Page News and Real-World Cues: A New Look at Agenda-Setting by the Media. *American Journal of Political Science* 24(1): 16-49.

Ericson, Richard V., Patricia M. Baranek, and Janet B.L. Chan. 1989. *Negotiating Control: A Study of News Sources*. Toronto: University of Toronto Press.

–. 1987. *Visualizing Deviance: A Study of News Organization*. Toronto: University of Toronto Press.

Eyal, Chaim E. 1981. The Roles of Newspapers and Television in Agenda-Setting. In *Mass Communication Review Yearbook*, vol. 2, edited by G. Cleveland Wilhoit and Harold de Bock. Beverly Hills, CA: Sage Publications.

Feige, Edgar L., and Douglas K. Pearce. 1979. The Causal Relationship Between Money and Income: Some Caveats for the Time Series Analysis. *Review of Econometrics and Statistics* 61: 521-33.

Ferejohn, John A., and Randall L. Calvert. 1984. Presidential Coattails in Historical Perspective. *American Journal of Political Science* 28(1): 127-46.

Fletcher, Frederick J. 1981. *The Newspaper and Public Affairs*. Research Publications, Royal Commission on Newspapers. Ottawa: Minister of Supply and Services Canada.

Fletcher, Joseph, and Paul Howe. 1999. Canadian Attitudes Toward the Charter and the Court: Results of a Recent IRPP Survey in Comparative Perspective. Paper presented at the Annual General Meeting of the Canadian Political Science Association, May, Sherbrooke, QC.

Flickinger, L.P. 1983. The Comparative Politics of Agenda Setting: The Emergence of Consumer Protection as a Public Policy Issue in Britain and the United States. *Policy Studies Review* 2: 429-44.

Fowler, J.S., and S.W. Showalter. 1974. Degree of Conformity in Lead Stories in Early Evening Network Newscasts. *Journalism Quarterly* 51: 712-15.

Franks, C.E.S. 1987. *The Parliament of Canada*. Toronto: University of Toronto Press.

Freeman, John R. 1983. Granger Causality and the Times Series Analysis of Political Relationships. *American Journal of Political Science* 27: 327-58.

Freeman, John R., Daniel Houser, Paul M. Kellstedt, and John T. Williams. 1998. Long-Memoried Processes, Unit Roots, and Causal Inference in Political Science. *American Journal of Political Science* 42(4): 1289-327.

Freeman, John R., John T. Williams, and Tse-min Lin. 1989. Vector Autoregression and the Study of Politics. *American Journal of Political Science* 33(4): 842-77.

Funkhouser, G. Ray. 1973. The Issues of the Sixties: An Exploratory Study in the Dynamics of Public Opinion. *Public Opinion Quarterly* 37: 62-75.

Funkhouser, G. Ray, and Eugene F. Shaw. 1990. How Synthetic Experience Shapes Social Reality. *Journal of Communication* 40(2): 75-87.

Gans, Herbert J. 1979. *Deciding What's News: A Study of CBS Evening News, NBC Nightly News, Newsweek, and* Time. New York: Pantheon Books.

Gilberg, Sheldon, Chaim Eyal, Maxwell McCombs, and David Nicholas. 1980. The State of the Union Address and the Press Agenda. *Journalism Quarterly* 57: 584-88.

Gilliam, Frank D., et al. 1996. Crime in Black and White: The Violent, Scary World of Local [US] News. *Harvard International Journal of Press/Politics* 1(3): 6-23.

Godfrey, L.G. 1978. Testing Against General Autoregressive and Moving Average Error Models When the Regressors Include Lagged Dependent Variables. *Econometrica* 46: 1293-302.

Gonzenbach, William J. 1992. A Time-Series Analysis of the Drug Issue, 1985-1990: The Press, the President and Public Opinion. *International Journal of Public Opinion Research* 4(2): 126-47.

–. 1996. *The Media, the President, and Public Opinion: A Longitudinal Analysis of the Drug Issue, 1984-1991*. Mahwah, NJ: Lawrence Erlbaum Associates.

Gonzenbach, William J., and Lee McGavin. 1997. A Brief History of Time: A Methodological Analysis of Agenda-Setting. In *Communication and Democracy: Exploring the Intellectual Frontiers in Agenda-Setting Theory,* edited by Maxwell E. McCombs, Donald L. Shaw, and David H. Weaver. Mahwah, NJ: Lawrence Erlbaum Associates.

Gordon, Donald. 1966. National News in Canadian Newspapers. Report presented to the Royal Commission on Bilingualism and Biculturalism.

Graber, Doris A. 1979. Is Crime News Coverage Excessive? *Journal of Communication* 29(3): 81-92.

Granger, C.W.J. 1969. Investigating Causal Relations by Econometric Models and Cross-Spectral Methods. *Econometrica* 37(3): 424-38.

Greene, W.H. 1992. *Econometric Analysis*. 2nd ed. New York: Macmillan.

Hale, Geoffrey E. 1998. Reforming Employment Insurance: Transcending the Politics of the Status Quo. *Canadian Public Policy* 24(4): 429-52.

Hall, Billy R. Jr., and Bryan D. Jones. 1997. Agenda Denial and Issue Containment in the Regulation of Financial Securities: The SEC, 1933-1995. In *Cultural Strategies of Agenda Denial: Avoidance, Attack, and Redefinition,* edited by Roger W. Cobb and Marc Howard Ross. Lawrence: University Press of Kansas.

Hansen, Anders. 1991. The Media and the Social Construction of the Environment. *Media, Culture and Society* 13(4): 443-58.

Hargrove, Erwin C., and Michael Nelson. 1984. *Presidents, Politics, and Policy.* Boston: Little, Brown.

Harman, Harry H. 1967. *Modern Factor Analysis*. 2nd ed. Chicago: University of Chicago Press.

Harrison, Kathryn. 1996. *Passing the Buck: Federalism and Environmental Policy.* Vancouver: University of British Columbia Press.

Hartley, Thomas, and Bruce Russet. 1992. Public Opinion and the Common Defense: Who Governs Military Spending in the United States? *American Political Science Review* 86(4): 905-15.

Harvey, Andrew C. 1981. *The Econometric Analysis of Time Series*. Oxford: Philip Allan.

Hatt, Ken, Tullio Caputo, and Barbara Perry. 1992. Criminal Justice Policy Under Mulroney: 1984-90: Neo-Conservatism, Eh? *Canadian Public Policy* 18(3): 245-60.

Hendry, David F. 1986. Econometric Modeling with Cointegrated Variables: An Overview. *Oxford Bulletin of Economics and Statistics* 48(3): 201-12.

–. 1995. *Dynamic Econometrics*. Oxford: Oxford University Press.

Herman, Edward S., and Noam Chomsky. 1988. *Manufacturing Consent: The Political Economy of the Mass Media*. New York: Pantheon Books.

Hertog, James K., John R. Finnegan Jr., and Emily Kahn. 1994. Media Coverage of AIDS, Cancer, and Sexually Transmitted Diseases: A Test of the Public Arenas Model. *Journalism Quarterly* 71(2): 291-304.

Hester, Al. 1978. Five Years of Foreign News on US Television Evening Newscasts. *Gazette* 24: 8695.

Hester, Joe Bob, and William J. Gonzenbach. 1995. The Environment: TV News, Real-World Cues, and Public Opinion Over Time. *Mass Communication Review* 22(1): 5-20.

Hilgartner, Stephen, and Charles L. Bosk. 1988. The Rise and Fall of Social Problems: A Public Arenas Model. *American Journal of Sociology* 94(1): 53-78.

Hill, David B. 1985. Viewer Characteristics and Agenda Setting by Television News. *Public Opinion Quarterly* 49(3): 340-50.

Hill, Kim Quaile. 1998. The Policy Agendas of the President and the Mass Public: A Research Validation and Extension. *American Journal of Political Science* 42: 1328-34.

Hinckley, Barbara. 1990. *The Symbolic Presidency: How Presidents Portray Themselves*. New York: Routledge.

Hoberg, George. 1991. Sleeping with an Elephant: The American Influence on Canadian Environmental Regulation. *Journal of Public Policy* 11(1): 107-32.

Hoberg, George, and Kathryn Harrison. 1994. It's Not Easy Being Green: The Politics of Canada's Green Plan. *Canadian Public Policy* 20(2): 119-37.

Hoff, John C. 1983. *A Practical Guide to Box-Jenkins Forecasting*. Belmont, CA: Lifetime Learning Publications.

Hoole, Francis W., and Chi Huang. 1992. The Political Economy of Global Conflict. *Journal of Politics* 54(3): 834-56.

Howlett, Michael. 1997. Issue-Attention and Punctuated Equilibria Models Reconsidered: An Empirical Examination of the Dynamics of Agenda-Setting in Canada. *Canadian Journal of Political Science* 30(1): 3-30.

–. 1998. Predictable and Unpredictable Policy Windows: Institutional and Exogenous Correlates of Canadian Federal Agenda-Setting. *Canadian Journal of Political Science* 31(3): 495-524.

Huegel, R., W. Degenhardt, and H. Weiss. 1989. Structural Equation Models for the Analysis of the Agenda-Setting Process. *European Journal of Communication* 4: 191-210.

Iyengar, Shanto, and Adam Simon. 1993. News Coverage of the Gulf Crisis and Public Opinion: A Study of Agenda-Setting, Priming, and Framing. *Communication-Research* 20(3): 365-83.

Iyengar, Shanto, and Donald R. Kinder. 1987. *News that Matters*. Chicago: University of Chicago Press.

Iyengar, Shanto, and Michael Suleiman. 1980. Trends in Public Support for Egypt and Israel, 1956-1978 [in the United States]. *American Politics Quarterly* 8: 34-60.

Iyengar, Shanto, Mark D. Peters, and Donald R. Kinder. 1983. Experimental Demonstrations of the "Not-So-Minimal" Consequences of Television News Programs. In *Mass Communication Review Yearbook*, vol. 4, edited by G. Cleveland. Beverly Hills, CA: Sage Publications.

Jackson, J. Edward. 1991. *A User's Guide to Principal Components*. New York: John Wiley and Sons.

Jasperson A.E., D.V. Shah, M. Watts, R.J. Faber, and D.P. Fan. 1998. Framing and the Public Agenda: Media Effects on the Importance of the Federal Budget Deficit. *Political Communication* 15(2): 205-24.

Jenkins, Richard W. 1999. Campaigns, the Media, and Insurgent Success: The Reform Party and the 1993 Canadian Election. Ph.D. dissertation, University of British Columbia.

Johnson, David R. 1997. Expected Inflation in Canada 1988-1995: An Evaluation of Bank of Canada Credibility and the Effect of Inflation Targets. *Canadian Public Policy* 23(3): 233-58.

Johnston, Richard. 1986. *Public Opinion and Public Policy in Canada: Questions of Confidence.* Toronto: University of Toronto Press.

Johnston, Richard, Andre Blais, Elisabeth Gidengil, and Neil Nevitte. 1996. *The Challenge of Direct Democracy: The 1992 Canadian Referendum.* Montreal: McGill-Queen's University Press.

Johnston, Richard, Andre Blais, Henry E. Brady, and Jean Crete. 1992. *Letting the People Decide: Dynamics of a Canadian Election.* Montreal and Kingston: McGill-Queen's University Press.

Jolliffe, I.T. 1986. *Principal Component Analysis.* New York: Springer-Verlag.

Jones, Bryan D. 1994. *Reconceiving Decision-Making in Democratic Politics: Attention, Choice, and Public Policy.* Chicago: University of Chicago Press.

Jones, Bryan D., Frank R. Baumgartner, and James L. True. 1998. Policy Punctuations: US Budget Authority, 1947-1995. *Journal of Politics* 60(1): 1-33.

Jones, Bryan D., James L. True, and Frank R. Baumgartner. 1997. Does Incrementalism Stem from Political Consensus or from Institutional Gridlock? *American Journal of Political Science* 41(1): 1319-39.

Judge, George C., R. Carter Hill, William E. Griffiths, Helmut Lutkepohl, and Lee Tsoung-Chao. 1988. *Introduction to the Theory and Practice of Econometrics.* 2nd ed. New York: John Wiley and Sons.

Kaye, Ronald. 1994. Defining the Agenda: British Refugee Policy and the Role of Parties. *Journal of Refugee Studies* 7(2-3): 144-59.

Kennedy, Peter. 1998. *A Guide to Econometrics.* 4th ed. Cambridge, MA: MIT Press.

Kessel, John H. 1974. Parameters of Presidential Politics. *Social Science Quarterly* 55: 8-24.

King, Gary. 1989. *Unifying Political Methodology: The Likelihood Theory of Statistical Inference.* Cambridge, UK: Cambridge University Press.

Kingdon, John W. 1995. *Agendas, Alternatives, and Public Policies.* 2nd ed. New York: HarperCollins.

Klapper, Joseph T. 1960. *The Effects of Mass Communication.* Glencoe, IL: The Free Press.

Kneebone, Ronald D. 1994. Deficits and Debt in Canada: Some Lessons from Recent History. *Canadian Public Policy* 20(2): 152-64.

Lang, Gladys Engel, and Kurt Lang. 1981. Watergate: An Exploration of the Agenda-Building Process. In *Mass Communication Review Yearbook,* vol. 2, edited by G. Cleveland Wilhoit and Harold de Bock. Beverly Hills, CA: Sage Publications.

Lawley, D.N., and A.E. Maxwell. 1971. *Factor Analysis as a Statistical Method.* 2nd ed. London: Butterworths.

Lewis-Beck, Michael S. 1980. *Applied Regression: An Introduction.* Beverly Hills, CA: Sage Publications.

Light, Paul C. 1993. Presidential Policy Making. In *Researching the Presidency: Vital Questions, New Approaches,* edited by George C. Edwards III, John H. Kessel, and Bert A. Rockman. Pittsburgh, PA: University of Pittsburgh Press.

–. 1999. *The President's Agenda.* 3rd ed. Baltimore: Johns Hopkins University Press.

Lindquist, Evert A., and David M. Rayside. 1992. Federal AIDS Policy for the 1990s: Is It Too Early for "Mainstreaming" in Canada? In *How Ottawa Spends: The Politics of Competitiveness, 1992-1993,* edited by Francis Abele. Ottawa: University of Carleton Press.

Lippmann, Walter. 1922. *Public Opinion.* New York: Macmillan.

Ljung, G.M., and G.E.P. Box. 1978. On a Measure of Lack of Fit in Time Series Models. *Biometrica* 65(2): 297-303.

MacKuen, Michael B., and Steven L. Coombs. 1981. *More Than News: Media Power in Public Affairs.* Beverly Hills, CA: Sage Publications.

MacKuen, Michael B., Robert S. Erikson, and James A. Stimson. 1992. Peasants or Bankers? The American Electorate and the US Economy. *American Political Science Review* 86(3): 597-611.

Maddala, G.S. 1988. *Introduction to Econometrics.* New York: Macmillan.

Maddala, G.S., and Kim, In-Moo. 1998. *Unit Roots, Cointegration, and Structural Change.* Cambridge, UK: Cambridge University Press.

March, Roman R. 1974. *The Myth of Parliament.* Scarborough, ON: Prentice Hall.

Matheson, W.A. 1976. *The Prime Minister and the Cabinet.* Toronto: Methuen.

Mayer, Robert N. 1991. Gone Yesterday, Here Today: Consumer Issues in the Agenda-Setting Process. *Journal of Social Issues* 47(1): 21-39.

McCleary, R., and R.A. Hay. 1980. *Applied Time Series Analysis for the Social Sciences.* Beverly Hills, CA: Sage Publications.

McCombs, Maxwell E., and Donald L. Shaw. 1972. The Agenda-Setting Function of the Mass Media. *Public Opinion Quarterly* 36(2): 176-85.

–. 1977. The Agenda-Setting Function of the Press. In *The Emergence of American Political Issues: The Agenda-Setting Function of the Press,* edited by Donald L. Shaw and Maxwell E. McCombs. St. Paul, MN: West Publishing.

–. 1993. The Evolution of Agenda-Setting Research: Twenty-Five Years in the Marketplace of Ideas. *Journal of Communication* 43(2): 58-67.

McCombs, Maxwell E., L. Danielian, and Wayne Wanta. 1995. Issues in the News and the Public Agenda: The Agenda-Setting Tradition. In *Public Opinion and the Communication of Consent,* edited by T.L. Glasser and C.T. Slamon. New York: Guilford.

McGuire, William J. 1986. The Myth of Massive Media Impact: Savagings and Salvagings. In *Political Communication and Behavior,* vol. 1, edited by George Comstock. New York: Academic Press.

Miller, Randy E., and Wayne Wanta. 1996. Sources of the Public Agenda: The President-Press-Public Relationship. *International Journal of Public Opinion Research* 8(4): 390-402.

Miller, Susan Heilmann. 1978. Reporters and Congressmen: Living in Symbiosis. *Journalism Monographs* 53.

Moen, Matthew C. 1990. Ronald Reagan and the Social Issues: Rhetorical Support for the Christian Right. *Social Science Journal* 27(2): 199-207.

Mollenhoff, Clark. 1965. *Tentacles of Power.* Cleveland: World.

Murray, Michael P. 1994. A Drunk and Her Dog: An Illustration of Cointegration and Error Correction. *American Statistician* 48(1): 37-40.

Neuman, W. Russell. 1990. The Threshold of Public Attention. *Public Opinion Quarterly* 54: 159-76.

Neuman, W. Russell, and Ann C. Fryling. 1985. Patterns of Political Cognition: An Exploration of the Public Mind. In *Mass Media and Political Thought: An Information-Processing Approach,* edited by Sidney Kraus and Richard M. Perloff. Beverly Hills, CA: Sage Publications.

Neuzil, Mark, and William Kovarik. 1996. *Mass Media and Environmental Conflict: America's Green Crusades.* Thousand Oaks, CA: Sage Publications.

Nevitte, Neil. 1996. *The Decline of Deference: Canadian Value Change in Cross-National Perspective.* Peterborough, ON: Broadview Press.

Normandeau, André. 1979. The Public and Violence: An Analysis of Crime Commission Reports; Le Public et la violence: l'analyse des rapports des commissions d'enquête. *Criminologie* 12(1): 81-88.

Olien, Clarice N., Phillip J. Tichenor, and George A. Donohue. 1989. Media Coverage and Social Movements. In *Information Campaigns: Balancing Social Values and Social Change,* edited by Charles T. Slamon. Newbury Park, CA: Sage Publications.

Page, Benjamin I., and Robert Y. Shapiro. 1983. Effects of Public Opinion on Policy. *American Political Science Review* 77: 175-90.

Parlour, J.W., and S. Schatzow. 1978. The Mass Media and Public Concern for Environmental Problems in Canada, 1960-1972. *International Journal of Environmental Studies* 13: 9-17.

Petry, François. 1995. The Party Agenda Model: Election Programmes and Government Spending in Canada. *Canadian Journal of Political Science* 28(1): 51-84.

–. 1999. The Opinion-Policy Relationship in Canada. *Journal of Politics* 61(2): 540-50.

Petry, François, Louis M. Imbeau, Jean Crête, and Michel Clavet. 1999. Electoral and Partisan Cycles in the Canadian Provinces. *Canadian Journal of Political Science* 32(2): 273-92.

Picard, Robert G., Maxwell McCombs, James P. Winter, and Stephen Lacy, eds. 1988. *Press Concentration and Monopoly.* Norwood, NJ: Ablex Publishing.

Pritchard, David. 1986. Homicide and Bargained Justice: The Agenda-Setting Effect of Crime News on Prosecutors. *Public Opinion Quarterly* 50(2): 143-59.

–. 1992. The News Media and Public Policy Agendas. In *Public Opinion, the Press, and Public Policy,* edited by J. David Kennamer. London: Praeger.

Pritchard, David, and Dan Berkowitz. 1993. The Limits of Agenda-Setting: The Press and Political Responses to Crime in the United States, 1950-1980. *International Journal of Public Opinion Research* 5(1): 86-91.

Pross, A. Paul. 1992. *Group Politics and Public Policy.* 2nd ed. Toronto: Oxford University Press.

Protess, David L., Fay Lomax Cook, Thomas R. Curtin, Margaret T. Gordon, Donna R. Leff, Maxwell E. McCombs, and Peter Miller. 1987. The Impact of Investigative Reporting on Public Opinion and Policymaking: Targeting Toxic Waste. *Public Opinion Quarterly* 51: 166-85.

Protess, David L., Donna R. Leff, Stephen C. Brooks, and Margaret T. Gordon. 1985. Uncovering Rape: The Watchdog Press and the Limits of Agenda Setting. *Public Opinion Quarterly* 49: 19-37.

Randall, Donna M., Lynette Lee Sammons, and Paul R. Hagner. 1988. Common Versus Elite Crime Coverage in Network News. *Social Science Quarterly* 69(4): 910-29.

Reese, Stephen, and Lucig H. Danielian. 1989. Intermedia Influence and the Drug Issue: Converging on Cocaine. In *Communication Campaigns About Drugs: Government, Media, and the Public,* edited by Pamela J. Shoemaker. Hillsdale, NJ: Lawrence Erlbaum Associates.

Riffe, D., B. Ellis, M.K. Rogers, R.L. Van Ommeren, and K.A. Woodman. 1986. Gatekeeping and the Network News Mix. *Journalism Quarterly* 63: 315-21.

Roberts, Alasdair, and Jonathan Rose. 1995. Selling the Goods and Services Tax: Government Advertising and Public Discourse in Canada. *Canadian Journal of Political Science* 28(2): 311-30.

Roberts, Marilyn S. 1992. Predicting Voting Behavior Via the Agenda-Setting Tradition. *Journalism Quarterly* 69(4): 878-92.

Rochefort, David A., and Roger W. Cobb, eds. 1994. *The Politics of Problem Definition: Shaping the Policy Agenda.* Lawrence: University Press of Kansas.

Rogers, Everett M., and James W. Dearing. 1988. Agenda-Setting Research: Where Has It Been, Where Is It Going? In *Communication Yearbook,* vol. 11, edited by James A. Anderson. London: Sage Publications.

Rogers, Everett M., James W. Dearing, and Dorine Bregman. 1993. The Anatomy of Agenda-Setting Research. *Journal of Communication* 43(2): 68-84.

Rogers, Everett M., James W. Dearing, and S. Chang. 1991. AIDS in the 1980s: The Agenda-Setting Process of a Public Issue. *Journalism Monographs* 126.

Rogers, Everett M., William B. Hart, and James W. Dearing. 1997. A Paradigmatic History of Agenda-Setting Research. In *Do the Media Govern? Politicians, Voters and Reporters in America,* edited by Shanto Iyengar and Richard Reeves. Thousand Oaks, CA: Sage Publications.

Rubin, David M., and David P. Sachs. 1973. *Mass Media and the Environment: Water Resources, Land Use and Atomic Energy in California.* New York: Praeger.

Rummel, R.J. 1970. *Applied Factor Analysis.* Evanston, IL: Northwestern University Press.

Savoie, Donald J. 1999. *Governing from the Centre: The Concentration of Power in Canadian Politics.* Toronto: University of Toronto Press.

–. 1990. *The Politics of Public Spending in Canada.* Toronto: University of Toronto Press.

Scheingold, S.A., and L.A. Gressett. 1987. Policy, Politics, and the Criminal Courts. *American Bar Foundation Research Journal* 2: 461-505.

Sharp, Elaine B. 1994. Paradoxes of National Antidrug Policymaking. In *The Politics of Problem Definition: Shaping the Policy Agenda,* edited by David A. Rochefort and Roger W. Cobb. Lawrence, KA: University Press of Kansas.

Shaw, Daniel, and Terrence J. Thomas. 1994. *Newspapers and Concentration.* Ottawa: Library of Parliament, Research Branch.

Shaw, Donald L., and Shannon E. Martin. 1992. The Function of Mass Media Agenda Setting. *Journalism Quarterly* 69(4): 902-20.

Shaw, Eugene F. 1977. The Interpersonal Agenda. In *The Emergence of American Political Issues: The Agenda-Setting Function of the Press,* edited by Donald L. Shaw and Maxwell E. McCombs. St. Paul, MN: West Publishing.

Sheley, Joseph F., and Cindy D. Ashkins. 1981. Crime, Crime News, and Crime Views. *Public Opinion Quarterly* 45(4): 492-506.

Shoemaker, J., Wayne Wanta, and D. Leggett. 1989. Drug Coverage and Public Opinion, 1972-1986. In *Communication Campaigns About Drugs: Government, Media, and the Public,* edited by P.J. Shoemaker. Hillsdale, NJ: Lawrence Erlbaum Associates.

Simeon, Richard, and David J. Elkins. 1980. Provincial Political Cultures in Canada. In *Small Worlds: Provinces and Parties in Canadian Political Life,* edited by David J. Elkins and Richard Simeon. Toronto: Methuen.

Simeon, Richard, and Donald E. Blake. 1980. Regional Preferences: Citizens' Views of Public Policy. In *Small Worlds: Provinces and Parties in Canadian Political Life,* edited by David J. Elkins and Richard Simeon. Toronto: Methuen.

Simeon, Richard, and E. Robert Miller. 1980. Regional Variations in Public Policy. In *Small Worlds: Provinces and Parties in Canadian Political Life,* edited by David J. Elkins and Richard Simeon. Toronto: Methuen.

Simon, Dennis M., Charles W. Ostrom Jr., and Robin F. Marra. 1991. The President, Referendum Voting, and Subnational Elections in the United States. *American Political Science Review* 85(4): 1177-92.

Sims, Christopher A. 1980. Macroeconomics and Reality. *Econometrica* 48(1): 1-48.

–. 1986. Are Forecasting Methods Usable for Policy Analysis? *Federal Reserve Bank of Minneapolis Quarterly Review* 10(1): 2-16.

Singer, Benjamin D. 1970. Violence, Protest and War in Television News: The US and Canada Compared. *Public Opinion Quarterly* 34(4): 611-16.

Smith, Kim A. 1987. Newspaper Coverage and Public Concern About Community Issues: A Time Series Analysis. *Journalism Monographs.*

Smith, Susan J. 1984. Crime in the News. *British Journal of Criminology* 24(3): 289-95.

Smith, Tom W. 1980. America's Most Important Problem – A Trend Analysis, 1946-1976. *Public Opinion Quarterly* 44: 164-80.

–. 1985. The Polls: America's Most Important Problems Part I: National and International. *Public Opinion Quarterly* 49: 264-74.

Soderlund, Walter C., Ronald H. Wagenberg, E. Donald Briggs, and Ralph C. Nelson. 1980a. Output and Feedback: Canadian Newspapers and Political Integration. *Journalism Quarterly* 57(2): 316-21.

–. 1980b. Regional and Linguistic Agenda-Setting in Canada: A Study of Newspaper Coverage of Issues Affecting Political Integration in 1976. *Canadian Journal of Political Science* 13(2): 347-56.

Sohn, Ardyth-Broadrick. 1978. A Longitudinal Analysis of Local Non-Political Agenda-Setting Effects. *Journalism Quarterly* 55(2): 325-33.

Soroka, Stuart. 1999a. Different Issues, Different Effects: Building an Issue Typology for Agenda-Setting. Paper presented at the Annual General Meeting of the Canadian Political Science Association, May, Sherbrooke, QC.

–. 1999b. Policy Agenda-Setting Theory Revisited: A Critique of Howlett on Downs, Baumgartner and Jones, and Kingdon. *Canadian Journal of Political Science* 32(4): 763-72.

–. 2000. Major Motion Pictures as Influential Media: Exploring the Media Agenda-Setting Capabilities of *Schindler's List. Canadian Journal of Communication* 25(2): 211-30.

–. 2001. What (and Where) Is the Most Important Problem? Paper presented at the Annual Meeting of the American Association of Public Opinion Research, May, Montreal, QC.

–. 2002a. Issue Attributes and Agenda-Setting: Media, the Public, and Policymakers in Canada. *International Journal of Public Opinion Research* (forthcoming).

–. 2002b. When Does News Matter? Public Agenda-Setting for Unemployment. Nuffield College Politics Working Paper 2002-W7.

Stempel, Guido H. III. 1985. Gatekeeping: The Mix of Topics and the Selection of Stories. *Journalism Quarterly* 62: 791-96.

Stone, Gerald C., and Maxwell E. McCombs. 1981. Tracing the Time Lag in Agenda-Setting. *Journalism Quarterly* 58: 51-55.

Sullivan, John L., L. Earl Shaw, Gregory E. McAvoy, and David G. Barnum. 1993. The Dimensions of Cue-Taking in the House of Representatives: Variation by Issue Area. *Journal of Politics* 55(4): 975-97.

Surlin, Stuart H. 1988. TV Network News: Canadian-American Comparison. *American Review of Canadian Studies* 18(4): 465-75.

Swanson, David L. 1988. Feeling the Elephant: Some Observations on Agenda-Setting Research. In *Communication Yearbook,* vol. 11, edited by James A. Anderson. London: Sage Publications.

Taras, David. 1990. *The Newsmakers: The Media's Influence on Canadian Politics.* Scarborough, ON: Nelson Canada.

–. 1999. *Power and Betrayal in the Canadian Media.* Peterborough, ON: Broadview Press.

Thiessen, Gordon G. 1998. The Canadian Experience with Targets for Inflation Control. *Canadian Public Policy* 34(4): 415-28.

Tremblay, Manon. 1998. Do Female MPs Substantively Represent Women? A Study of Legislative Behaviour in Canada's 35th Parliament. *Canadian Journal of Political Science* 31(3): 435-65.

Vermaeten, Arndt, W. Irwin Gillespie, and Frand Vermaeten. 1995. Who Paid the Taxes in Canada, 1951-1988? *Canadian Public Policy* 21(3): 317-43.

Wagenberg, Ronald H., and Walter C. Soderlund. 1976. The Effects of Chain Ownership on Editorial Coverage: The Case of the 1974 Canadian Federal Election. *Canadian Journal of Political Science* 9(4): 682-89.

–. 1975. The Influence of Chain Ownership on Editorial Comment in Canada. *Journalism Quarterly* 52: 93-98.

Walcott, Charles E., and Karen M. Hult. 1995. *Governing the White House from Hoover through LBJ.* Lawrence: University Press of Kansas.

Wanta, Wayne. 1988. The Effects of Dominant Photographs: An Agenda-Setting Experiment. *Journalism Quarterly* 65: 107-11.

–. 1997. *The Public and the National Agenda: How People Learn About Important Issues.* Mahwah, NJ: Lawrence Erlbaum Associates.

Wanta, Wayne, and Yi-Chen Wu. 1992. Interpersonal Communication and the Agenda-Setting Process. *Journalism Quarterly* 69(4): 847-55.

Wanta, Wayne, and Yu-Wei Hu. 1993. The Agenda-Setting Effects of International News Coverage: An Examination of Differing News Frames. *International Journal of Public Opinion Research* 5(3): 250-64.

–. 1994. The Effects of Credibility, Reliance, and Exposure on Media Agenda-Setting: A Path Analysis Model. *Journalism Quarterly* 71: 90-98.

–. 1994. Time-Lag Differences in the Agenda-Setting Process: An Examination of Five News Media. *International Journal of Public Opinion Research* 6(3): 225-40.

Wanta, Wayne, M. Stephenson, J.V. Turk, and M.E. McCombs. 1989. How the President's State of the Union Talk Influenced News Media Agendas. *Journalism Quarterly* 66(3): 537-41.

Watt, James H., Mary Mazza, and Leslie Snyder. 1993. Agenda-Setting Effects of Television News Coverage and the Effects Decay Curve. *Communication Research* 20(3): 408-35.

Watt, James H., and Sjef van den Berg. 1981. How Time Dependency Influences Media Effects in a Community Controversy. *Journalism Quarterly* 58: 43-50.

Weaver, D.H., M.E. McCombs, and C. Spellman. 1975. Watergate and the Media: A Case Study in Agenda-Setting. *American Politics Quarterly* 3: 458-72.

Weaver, David H. 1991. Issue Salience and Public Opinion: Are There Consequences of Agenda-Setting? *International Journal of Public Opinion Research* 3(1): 53-68.

–. 1977. Political Issues and Voter Need for Orientation. In *The Emergence of American Political Issues: The Agenda-Setting Function of the Press,* edited by D.L Shaw and Maxwell E. McCombs. St. Paul, MN: West Publishing.

Weaver, David H., Jian-Hua Zhu, and Lars Willnat. 1992. The Bridging Function of Interpersonal Communication in Agenda-Setting. *Journalism Quarterly* 69(4): 856-67.

Weiss, Carol H. 1974. What America's Leaders Read. *Public Opinion Quarterly* 38(1): 1-22.

Wildavsky, Aaron. 1964. *The Politics of the Budgetary Process.* Boston: Little, Brown.

Wilkerson, John D., T. Jens Feeley, Nicole S. Schiereck, and Christi Sue. 1999. Policy Interest and Legislative Responsiveness: Bill Introductions as Indicators of Issue Salience. Paper presented at the Annual Meeting of the American Political Science Association, August-September, Atlanta, GA.

Wilson, Jeremy. 1981. Media Coverage of Canadian Election Campaigns: Horse-Race Journalism and the Meta-Campaign. *Journal of Canadian Studies* 15: 56-68.

Winter, James P. 1981. Contingent Conditions in the Agenda-Setting Process. In *Mass Communication Review Yearbook,* vol. 2, edited by G. Cleveland Wilhoit and Harold de Bock. Beverly Hills, CA: Sage Publications.

–. 1997. *Democracy's Oxygen: How Corporations Control the News.* Montreal: Black Rose Books.

Winter, James P., and Chaim H. Eyal. 1981. Agenda Setting for the Civil Rights Issue. *Public Opinion Quarterly* 45(3): 376-83.

Winter, James P., Chaim H. Eyal, and Ann H. Rogers. 1982. Issue Specific Agenda-Setting: The Whole Is Less Than the Sum of the Parts. *Canadian Journal of Communication* 8: 1-10.

Wlezien, Christopher. 2001. On the Salience of Political Issues. Paper presented at the Annual Meeting of the Midwest Political Science Association, April, Chicago, IL.

Yagade, Aileen, and David M. Dozier. 1990. The Media Agenda-Setting Effect of Concrete Versus Abstract Issues. *Journalism Quarterly* 67(1): 3-10.

Zellner, Arnold. 1962. An Efficient Method of Estimating Seemingly Unrelated Regressions and Tests for Aggregation Bias. *Journal of the American Statistical Association* 57: 348-68.

Zhu, Jian-Hua. 1992. Issue Competition and Attention Distraction: A Zero-Sum Theory of Agenda-Setting. *Journalism Quarterly* 69: 825-36.

Zhu, Jian-Hua, and William Boroson. 1997. Susceptibility to Agenda Setting: A Cross-Sectional and Longitudinal Analysis of Individual Differences. In *Communication and Democracy: Exploring the Intellectual Frontiers in Agenda-Setting Theory,* edited by Maxwell E. McCombs, Donald L. Shaw, and David H. Weaver. Mahwah, NJ: Lawrence Erlbaum Associates.

Zhu, Jian Hua, James H. Watt, Leslie B. Snyder, Jingtao Yan, and Yansong Jiang. 1993. Public Issue Priority Formation: Media Agenda-Setting and Social Interaction. *Journal of Communication* 43(1): 8-29.

Zucker, Harold G. 1978. The Variable Nature of News Media Influence. In *Communication Yearbook,* vol. 2, edited by B.D. Ruben. New Brunswick, NJ: Transaction Books.

Index

Set in Stone by Artegraphica Design Co. Ltd.

Printed and bound in Canada by Friesens

Copy editor: Frank Chow

Proofreader: Viola Funk